Chinese Literature: A Very Short Introduction

VERY SHORT INTRODUCTIONS are for anyone wanting a stimulating and accessible way in to a new subject. They are written by experts and have been published in more than 25 languages worldwide.

The series began in 1995 and now represents a wide variety of topics in history, philosophy, religion, science, and the humanities. The VSI library now contains 300 volumes—a Very Short Introduction to everything from ancient Egypt and Indian philosophy to conceptual art and cosmology—and will continue to grow in a variety of disciplines.

Very Short Introductions available now:

Available soon:

For more information visit our website

www.oup.co.uk/general/vsi/

Sabina Knight

CHINESE LITERATURE

A Very Short Introduction

OXFORD
UNIVERSITY PRESS

Oxford University Press, Inc., publishes works that further
Oxford University's objective of excellence
in research, scholarship, and education.

Oxford   New York
Auckland   Cape Town   Dar es Salaam   Hong Kong   Karachi
Kuala Lumpur   Madrid   Melbourne   Mexico City   Nairobi
New Delhi   Shanghai   Taipei   Toronto

With offices in
Argentina   Austria   Brazil   Chile   Czech Republic   France   Greece
Guatemala   Hungary   Italy   Japan   Poland   Portugal   Singapore
South Korea   Switzerland   Thailand   Turkey   Ukraine   Vietnam

Copyright © 2012 by Oxford University Press, Inc.

Published by Oxford University Press, Inc.
198 Madison Avenue, New York, NY 10016

www.oup.com

Library of Congress Cataloging-in-Publication Data
Knight, Sabina, 1966–
Chinese literature : a very short introduction / Sabina Knight.
p.   cm.
Includes bibliographical references and index.
ISBN 978-0-19-539206-7 (pbk.)
1. Chinese literature—History and criticism. I. Title.
PL2265.K65 2012
895.1′09—dc23   2011031587

1 3 5 7 9 8 6 4 2

Printed in Great Britain
by Ashford Colour Press Ltd., Gosport, Hants.
on acid-free paper

For Joseph S. M. Lau, my teacher

Contents

List of illustrations

Preface

"Climbing Stork Tower" 登鸛雀樓

Wang Zhihuan 王之渙 (688–742)

白日依山盡
黃河入海流
欲窮千里目
更上一層樓

Sunlight reclines on the mountains and ends;
The Yellow River flows on, to the sea.
If [you] desire to see all of a thousand leagues,
Come up another flight of the tower [with me].

This eighth-century poem recalls the traditional Chinese view of culture as a continuous river. Although full of bends and tributaries, this powerful river has nourished the inhabitants of what is now called China for more than three thousand years. Chinese thinkers have long sought to discern the principles of this vast flow, and their understandings have in turn shaped the river's course. Belief in cycles of chaos and order, conflict and resolution, for example, may have inspired the four-part structure of regulated quatrains whereby four lines begin, continue, turn, and resolve the poem's theme. In Wang's poem, this neat pattern offers a view of a vast horizon, and, despite a tinge of sadness over the sun's disappearance, the poem ends with encouraging words. Best seen from a height, the river's twists and turns form a meaningful course.

This book tells the story of Chinese literature, from antiquity to the present, in terms of the central role literary culture has played in supporting social and political concerns. Taking literary culture as a collective effort to navigate the flow of experience, the book approaches Chinese literature as a vast river of dynamic human passions, especially moral and sensual passions, and of aesthetic practices for cultivating and regulating those passions. The major traditions of Chinese thought share a conviction that much distress results from failures of perspective, and that literature can open people's eyes, minds, and hearts.

China's earliest records present literary culture as fundamental to steering good government and promoting social betterment. To illustrate the close tie between aesthetics and ethical teachings, this book foregrounds the genres of lyric and narrative, and also touches upon philosophy, history, and drama. Since a more restricted concept of literature developed only in the late nineteenth century, this scope honors traditional Chinese culture's broader understanding of literature, history, and thought as parts of a whole.

In Chinese contexts, the study of literature nurtured devotion to this larger whole. To understand dynamic processes of change, literature addressed nature's cycles of vigor and exhaustion. Such attention fostered literary theories that placed individual writers, movements, and the rise and fall of genres within a larger landscape formed by shifting winds of historical and natural processes. As the regulated poetry of the Tang dynasty lost favor, the genre gave way to lyrics and arias; as verse as a whole declined, narration rose. Such theories often attributed to cultural developments a life of their own, but the story of Chinese literature is also a story of its service to specific interests. Elite patronage played a powerful role, and habits of transmission and canonization tended to serve those interests. Reading individual works brings the pleasure of gazing at reflections on the surface of the river. To see the depths below means addressing not only questions of language and cross-cultural understanding but also dynamics of power, including class, gender, ethnicity, and nationalism.

Interweaving general themes with specific examples, the book introduces its principal concerns as conversations between texts. This comparative method allows sensitivity to crosscurrents and undercurrents as well as dominant directions. It also underscores the syncretism and diversity within China's literary traditions. What does it mean to be human? How might benevolent people convey the Way, express feelings, tell stories, entertain and influence one another, and develop a humane society? The perspectives offered in Chinese literature are eminently relevant to present ethical, aesthetic, social, and environmental concerns, and this book aims to empower readers to enter and further these conversations. Following the sage Confucius (551–479 BCE), who trusted his students to complete the square once he held up one corner, this rough sketch offers a guidebook through the vast landscape of Chinese literature. Though much remains to be explored, these glimpses of a powerful tradition may inspire the reader to continue, just as Wang's poem emboldens his listener to ascend another story.

Acknowledgments and credits

This book was an unanticipated labor of love, and I am grateful to Nancy Toff and Jeffrey Wasserstrom for proposing it. Many teachers shaped my understandings of classical and modern Chinese and their literatures, and I am especially indebted to Cyril Birch, Tsai-fa Cheng, Samuel H. N. Cheung, Robert Joe Cutter, William H. Nienhauser, and, above all, Joseph S. M. Lau. Vicky Knight and Samuel A. Richmond closely edited, and Lev Navarre Chao offered perceptive suggestions from a student's view. For helpful comments and discussion, I also thank Michael Puett, Kidder Smith, and anonymous readers for Oxford University Press. Finally, deepest thanks go to Wilson Chao for his great faith, incisive editorial advice, and love of clear writing.

Credits

Chapter 1
Foundations: ethics, parables, and fish

The paths to knowledge in Chinese literature may sometimes surprise. Readers sympathetic to intuitive understanding will find inspiration in the collection named after the legendary sage Zhuangzi 莊子 (lit., "Master Zhuang," ca. 369–286 BCE). Here is Zhuangzi's conversation with the logician Huizi as they wander on a bridge above the Hao River.

> "The fish swim at ease, for they are happy."
> "You're not a fish," says Huizi. "How do you know the fish are happy?"
> "You're not me. How do you know that I do not know that the fish are happy?"
> "I am not you; surely I do not know you. You surely are not a fish; thus you do not know that the fish are happy."
> "Please let me trace back to the root of this," Zhuangzi continues. "The reason you asked how I know the fish are happy is that you already knew that I knew. I know it just by being here above the Hao."

Zhuangzi first engages Huizi's logic, but then offers another path to wisdom. Just as Huizi could know what Zhuangzi knew even if he did not agree, Zhuangzi sensed that the fish were happy. For the logician, language is the only means of communication. For Zhuangzi, since he and the fish are part of the same universe, he can be attuned to the fish. To be so attuned means continually broadening one's perspective, as the River Spirit learns in another parable attributed to Zhuangzi. Having journeyed to the ocean, the River Spirit realizes he has seen but part of the whole. The Ocean Spirit comments, "You cannot speak of the ocean to a well-frog."

The desire for a broader perspective, shared by all the major schools of Chinese thought, is memorably voiced by one of China's most beloved poets, the optimistic statesman Su Shi 蘇軾 (1037–1101). In "First Rhyme-prose on a Red Cliff" 前赤壁賦, Su describes a boat outing on the Yangtze River. The drinking party turns somber when they pass a famous battle site. Because defeat at this site effectively sealed the downfall of the Han dynasty, the visit inspires a dialogue on questions of change and continuity. How can one make sense of the destruction of former kingdoms? At one point a guest laments the insignificance of human existence.

> [Like] mayflies thrown between heaven and earth.
> One grain in a boundless green sea.

To assuage his friend's anxiety, Su evokes the moon that waxes and wanes and rivers that flow on and on but never disappear. Recalling nature's constancy, he encourages a more philosophical attitude toward change.

> If you view things from the aspect of change,
> Then heaven and earth can last no longer than the blink of an eye.
> But if you view things from their unchanging aspect,
> Then material things and I will never end.

Su's eleventh-century reflections on impermanence and constancy address a guiding theme of the Chinese literary imagination. How can one respond to the transient nature of human existence? Concern about time's passing added urgency to questions of benefit and harm, imperatives of public service, and desires for friendship, family, and other achievements. Literary culture helped people pursue these questions and desires, and this focus on human pursuits guided them in facing the changes wrought by time. *Zuo's Commentary* 左傳 of the late fourth century BCE documents this reliance on words as one of three ways "to die but not to perish": First is to establish virtue; second to establish good deeds, and third to establish words.

Conveying the Way: the power of patterns

The antiquity of early Chinese texts is astounding by Western standards. Although modern Chinese differs from early Chinese as much as English differs from Latin, experts today can still read the Chinese inscribed on tortoise shells and sheep scapulae dating from the Shang dynasty (1600–1046 BCE). Used for divination, these oracle bone inscriptions asked questions composed of individual characters (*zi* 字), the answers to which were divined by interpreting cracks formed when the bones were heated over fire.

These characters became the foundation of Chinese culture. Although their forms and meanings evolved over time, modern Chinese still uses characters from ancient texts, and the continuity of the writing system has been crucial in helping China's central traditions to cohere. The writing system's uniformity across the continent has also enabled communication despite wide variations among the spoken languages of different regions. Often called "dialects," but better named "topolects" (languages of places), many of these regional languages are as different orally as German from English.

China's survival over three thousand years may owe more to its literary traditions than to its political history. Unlike the Roman Empire, China repeatedly reunited as a polity in part through faith in the power of writing (*wen* 文), and written Chinese played a key role in sustaining a tension-ridden yet resilient civilization. A peaceful counterpart to the military realm, writing was seen as the root of civil practice, an indispensable means to nourish

3

1. Early Chinese characters can be seen on this "oracle bone inscription" carved on a tortoise shell (ca. 1300–1050 BCE).

cultural harmony. The end of Lu Ji's 陸機 third-century "Rhyme-prose on Literature" 文賦 praises writing's power to serve as a bridge across time: "Looking down, it bequeaths patterns to the future; gazing up, it contemplates the examples of the ancients."

More than merely a mirror of an already existing world or of ideal forms, literature was understood to be a tangible means by which the world comes to be. The patterns of writing were thought to be concrete forms of the principle (*li* 理) of natural structures, and so writing played a key role in passing on the natural and moral Way (*Dao* 道).

Crafted writing thus promoted faith in an ordered and moral universe. The power of this ideal, later captured in the proverbial "Texts serve to convey the Way," explains the central role accorded written texts and the scholars who commented on them. The sage Confucius encouraged his disciples to study writing whenever strength remained after fulfilling moral duties, and this study was seen as fundamental to education for public service.

Though "the study of writing" (*wenxue* 文學) later becomes the Chinese term for literature, the term *wen* refers etymologically to a pattern, as in a woven fabric. Closer to the idea of the liberal arts, *wen* can refer to any patterned art form, and "carefully patterned writing" well describes literature's broad scope in early China. The ancient Greco-Roman world saw liberal arts as the education proper to a free man, and Confucian scholars saw the study of writing as essential to the cultivation of human-heartedness. To access the inherent order of the universe, no priests or other intermediaries were necessary, but people needed teachers and texts.

The literati

Perhaps nowhere else in the world has literature been as conscious a collective endeavor as in China. Reading and writing integrated individuals in an enduring stream of humanity, and members of the scholar-official class bore their privilege as a heavy responsibility. Because the Way of nature and of moral conduct was thought to lie in recurrent patterns, emphasis on recognizing patterns fostered a strong historical consciousness.

The importance of historical reflection grew during the decline of the Zhou dynasty (1027–256 BCE). As the development of iron revolutionized warfare, during the Warring States period (475–221 BCE) well-armed feudal states annexed their neighbors until the northern state of Qin established China's first unified dynasty (221–207 BCE). (The English word "China" comes from Qin.)

One key to the Qin's success was its development of a bureaucracy of able scholars granted official positions. As this new class of educated gentry sought political influence, the Qin forged a bond between written culture and politics that would last until the late twentieth century. For most of the thirteen centuries between 605 and 1905, governments reinforced this bond by recruiting officials through an examination system based on classical literary study.

The difficulty of classical Chinese restricted literacy to this elite scholar-official class. Learning to read and write required tutoring, time, and access to books that were economically feasible only for a very limited group. Until the Song dynasty (960–1279), when printing enabled a great increase in literacy, most writers were part of the government bureaucracy. These scholars read a fairly stable canon of works, and their shared education made the scholar-official class more cohesive and powerful than any analogous group elsewhere. Scholars depended on the patronage of rulers, and rulers relied on scholars' commentaries on the classics to bolster the legitimacy of their reigns.

The classics

Despite the "bibliocaust" in which the first emperor of the Qin dynasty (r. 221–210 BCE) burned books other than legal and essential professional texts, many works of pre-Qin literature survive, thanks to their preservation in those historical works that were spared burning. The designation of select texts as "classics" (*jing* 經) promoted the prestige of these early writings. These classics evolved through the accretion of commentaries, most of which interpreted earlier texts in order to legitimate given rulers or political orientations.

Since the Han dynasty (206 BCE–220 CE) the "Five Classics" refer to a divination manual, the *Classic of Changes* 易經; the oldest anthology of poems, the *Classic of Poetry* 詩經; a collection of speeches and decrees, the *Classic of Documents* 書經; a historical chronicle, the *Springs and Autumns* 春秋; and three handbooks of rules for behavior named together as the *Ritual* 禮. Thanks to the invention of paper (second century BCE), these classics were carved in stone to produce rubbings and memorized by almost all educated Chinese.

A broader sense of authoritative writings came with the fourth-century division of texts into four main categories. This taxonomy made classics primary and history secondary, followed by the "masters" (thinkers later called philosophers), and collections of belles lettres. Rich in aphorisms, lively dialogues, fables and anecdotes, texts in the "masters" category were usually composites of later date that collected a given master's dialogues with disciples or opponents. The rubric also included professional medical, military, and religious texts, including the Daoist and Buddhist canons. Texts that would later be labeled fiction did not generally merit inclusion in any of these categories, all centrally concerned with conveying the Way.

Debates about the Way had taken shape during the pre-Qin period when the lack of a political center permitted the rise of professional thinkers and diplomats. As these concerned scholars sought to persuade rulers of better paths to peace and good government, those unable to serve as officials often became teachers of disciples. These thinkers made the Warring States China's richest period of philosophical debate, a time famous for its "Hundred Schools of Thought." Of these schools, the historian Sima Tan 司馬談 (d. 110 BCE) identified six that, thanks in part to his formulation, would come to have a sustained influence. In addition to identifying as schools the Naturalists 陰陽家, Confucians 儒家, and Moists 墨家, Sima invented the categories of Legalists 法家, Logicians 名家 ("Sophists," lit., the "School of Names"), and Daoists 道家.

Buddhism, too, would soon contribute profoundly to debates about the path of right living. Originally from India, Buddhism became a major branch of Chinese thought, and Buddhist stories from India were among the earliest fictional works in China. By the second century, poetic renderings of the life of Sakyamuni Buddha and other Buddhist parables were translated into Chinese, and these parables and *sutras* (threads) became essential elements of the literary tradition. (The esteemed term for "classics" [*jing* 經] was also used for *sutra* titles.) Often synthesized with Confucian and Daoist ideas, Buddhist concepts of illusion, predestined union, karma, and reincarnation soon took root as folk beliefs; beliefs with especially wide appeal during the disunion following the collapse of the Han dynasty in 220. By the Tang dynasty (617–907), when a reunited China expanded militarily and welcomed broader dealings with foreign ideas and people, Buddhist themes and forms had influenced many major developments in Chinese literature. Understanding of this influence was revolutionized by the early twentieth-century unearthing of almost 40,000 manuscripts from a cave sealed since the eleventh century near Dunhuang in western China.

Despite different emphases, these major schools of thought shared many overlapping beliefs, including belief in an ultimate Way of harmony grounded in the unity of heaven, earth, and humanity. Each school saw the others' teachings not as wrong but as possessing only a partial understanding of the greater whole. As centuries of debate and cross-fertilization created an evolving syncretism, these schools' shared concerns became major currents in the literary tradition. The foundations of Chinese literature can be mapped as overlapping paths for approaching the Way.

The Way of change

Chinese language and literature possess a rich vocabulary for exploring the subtle operations of change. Whereas Indo-European languages often privilege nouns, essences, and substances, classical Chinese privileges verbs, processes, and situations. Seeing historical transformations as fulfillments of

2. Among the discoveries near Dunhuang was the world's oldest known printed book, the woodblock *Diamond Sutra* 金剛經 of 868 CE.

more gradual processes of change, Chinese literature frequently resists precise definitions and static categories.

This emphasis on change is as ancient as the *Classic of Changes*, a work that began as a divination manual early in the first millennium BCE. From ancient roots in "fortune telling," the text evolved into one of world literature's most important wisdom books (one of few known in English by its Chinese name, *I Ching [Yi jing]*).

The core of the classic gives sixty-four short prophecies each corresponding to a diagram of six lines called a hexagram. Composed of solid lines (*yang* 陽) signifying movement, and broken lines (*yin* 陰) signifying yielding and rest, the hexagrams represent stages in the cycles and sequences of a cosmos that, thanks to such patterns, could be seen as ultimately tending toward order. These sixty-four hexagrams, metaphors for life's crucial transitions, offered a symbolic universe through which an individual might comprehend his predicaments, or an emperor might reckon opportunities of statecraft.

Wind	風	䷺		渙
Water	水			Dispersion

3. "Dispersion" (*huan* 渙), the fifty-ninth of the sixty-four hexagrams, is composed of the trigram for "wind" over the trigram for "water." The hexagram might be interpreted to suggest the dissolution of rigidity, or the letting go of regret.

The *Changes'* first two hexagrams, heaven, or the creative (*Qian* 乾), and earth, or the receptive (*Kun* 坤) correspond to the primal *yang* 陽 and the primal *yin* 陰, characters whose root meanings refer to the sunny and shady sides of a hill. As light and shade mingle on a hillside, the stimulating *yang* and responsive *yin* interact according to natural contingencies. Although beyond human control, these contingencies were seen to follow regular patterns. Sensitivity to these dynamics fostered awe for the potentials underlying natural dispositions (*shi* 勢), plus profound faith in human capacities to navigate these propensities. Here, for example, is the text's judgment of the situation symbolized by the second hexagram:

> THE RECEPTIVE brings about sublime success,
> Furthering through the perseverance of a mare.
> If the superior man undertakes something and tries to lead,
> He goes astray;
> But if he follows, he finds guidance.
> It is favorable to find friends in the west and south,
> To forego friends in the east and north.
> Quiet perseverance brings good fortune.

Because such judgments on evolving propensities and long-term consequences allowed a measure of freedom from immediate impulses and pressures, the *Changes* established a paradigm for written culture's power to provide ethical guidance.

The *Changes* ends with appendices known as the "Ten Wings." Though traditionally attributed to Confucius, these appendices apply naturalistic theories that date after his life, closer to the third century BCE. According to these theories, the ceaseless interaction of *yin* and *yang* generates *qi* 氣, the life force of the universe made tangible in breath, air, energy, and matter. This vital force cycles through five phases of metal, wood, water, fire, and earth. To these five phases are correlated the five viscera, the five colors, the five odors, and the five notes of the Chinese musical scale. On a principle of resonance 感應 (lit., "stimulus and response"), happenings in one domain affect corresponding agents of the same "category" 類 in other domains. This correlative cosmology, called "*yinyang* five agents" 陰陽五行, fostered regard for dynamic ecosystems and encouraged flexibility in drawing on diverse schools of thought. Just as the balance of *yin* and *yang* changes with the seasons, governments could employ different policies at different times.

These holistic beliefs inspired appreciation for cycles of order and disorder, and sensitivity to the interplay of hard and soft, stillness and movement, silence and speech, the hidden and the visible. Just as joy and sorrow intermingle, the direct and indirect fit different situations. This principle is reprised in discussions of confrontation in Sunzi's 孫子 *Art of War* 孫子兵法 (ca. fourth century BCE), in physical practices of *taiji* and *qigong*, in theories of hot and cold in Chinese medicine, and in the emphasis on suggestion and indirectness in Chinese poetry.

The received *Classic of Changes* was also shaped by influential Daoist and Confucian commentaries, interpretations that made its profound reverence for nature's changes a major current in Chinese thought. Buddhist insights into impermanence furthered these earlier schools' appreciation of change, an influence particularly evident in landscape poetry. In such poetry, as in certain genres of prose, the use of grammatical and semantic parallelism often reflects the correlative patterns. This framework

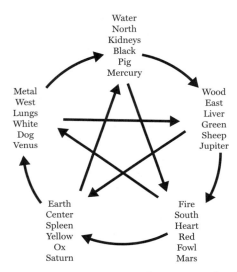

Water
North
Kidneys
Black
Pig
Mercury

Metal
West
Lungs
White
Dog
Venus

Wood
East
Liver
Green
Sheep
Jupiter

Earth
Center
Spleen
Yellow
Ox
Saturn

Fire
South
Heart
Red
Fowl
Mars

4. This chart shows various phenomena that correspond to the "Five Agents" through whose phases the vital *qi* force circulates.

can be seen even in short "broken line" quatrains that encapsulate the brevity of human perception. In Li Shangyin's 李商隱 (813–58) "On Merry-Making Plain" 登樂遊原, for example, the "toward evening" of the first line invokes the movement of time beyond human control, whereas the second line's "driving carriage" names movement through space within the speaker's influence.

> Toward evening my mood is not quite right.
> Driving a carriage and ascending the ancient plain.
> The evening sun is limitlessly beautiful,
> It is only that dusk is near.

Similarly, the closing invocation of dusk echoes the "toward evening" of the opening to create a circular movement reminiscent of the sun's daily return. Yet dusk's approach also suggests the insignificance of the speaker, especially as the boundlessness of the sunset's beauty underlines a contrast with the many limits of human existence. In this way, the poem's focus on concrete scenery expresses intangible feeling. The speaker's sadness at the end of a beautiful day resonates with a sense of his own mortality and perhaps of foreboding concerning the dynasty's decline.

The Way of benevolence

Alongside these naturalist theories, China also developed a powerful tradition of ethical humanism. First expounded by Confucius 孔子 (lit., "Master Kong," 551–479 BCE), this classical tradition was developed by a group of scholars (*ru* 儒) who saw themselves as his inheritors. Given the great value this "Rujia" 儒家 school put on following tradition to foster harmony and stability, rather than "Confucianism," as it came to be known in the West, this school might better be called "traditionalism."

In the *Analects* 論語, a record of short sayings and conversations probably compiled in the third century BCE, Confucius speaks to pragmatic considerations of benefit and harm. Although not a systematic treatise, this influential source of the master's teachings presents a judicious thinker dedicated to goodness and sincerity. Ready to admit not knowing as half of knowledge, Confucius declines to speak about anomalies, spirits, or life after death in favor of addressing this-worldly matters he could know. In contrast to the Naturalists and Daoists, who exalted nature's Way, Confucius and his followers emphasized the moral Way of harmonious human relations. Troubled by the strife and moral decline of his own era, Confucius looked to history and especially venerated the Duke of Zhou.

Confucius made the Duke of Zhou's concept of benevolence (*ren* 仁) central to his teachings. Sometimes translated as "human-heartedness," or simply "humanity," *ren* combines the root "person" 人 with the number two 二, an etymology that reflects Confucius's conviction that cultivated humanity depends on interaction with others. For Confucius, family relations and filial piety were the building blocks, the center from which one could extend benevolence to others. "A person of humanity, wishing to be established, also establishes others, and wishing to succeed, also helps others to succeed." Asked whether one word could guide action throughout life, Confucius proposed reciprocity as the most dependable guide. "Is not reciprocity such a word? Do not do to others what you would not want done to you."

For Confucius, the goal of a cultivated gentleman was to promote social and political order by following early Zhou rules of courtesy and ritual. Music and literary culture were essential to ritual interaction, and first and foremost in developing virtue was to accord words and actions, what Confucius called "rectifying the names." Confucian teachings thus grant a powerful place to the literary arts in the cultivation of moral virtues. Confucius appreciated the musical qualities of the *Classic of Poetry*, and he repeatedly invoked the poems as valuable for moral and rhetorical training: "If one does not study poetry, one will be without the means to speak." Nor did Confucius see learning the moral Way as a dreary affair: "To know it is not as good as to love it, and to love it is not as good as to take delight in it."

Mencius 孟子 (372–289 BCE) promoted even greater optimism about people's power to better their world through the cultivation of benevolence, moral courage, and ritual propriety. The *Mencius*, the text named for him, was as influential as the *Analects* in initiating the tradition that later become known as Confucianism. Holding that all people have "four hearts"—compassion, dutifulness, ritual propriety, and a sense of right and wrong, Mencius linked these virtues to "the flood-like *qi*," the vital energy that could fuel moral courage. For Mencius, the common impulse to save a child from falling into a well and the inability to bear the suffering of others demonstrate that human nature tends to do good as naturally as water flows downward.

Confucius's follower Xunzi 荀子 (ca. 300–230 BCE) disputed Mencius's contention that people were inherently good. Seeing people as by nature asocial, partial to their loved ones, and even selfish, he believed that only education and ritual could lead them to acquire goodness and behave harmoniously in society. Xunzi's skepticism about humanity's inherent goodness led to an emphasis on rules developed by Han Feizi 韓非子 (d. 233 BCE). Seeing morality as too shaky a basis for regulating behavior, Master Han Fei advocated developing a system of laws and strong bureaucratic institutions that would lead to the intellectual tradition later known as Legalism. Yet even the sayings in the *Xunzi* and the systems of the legalists recognize historical precedents as providing values and norms of conduct, and this vision underpins these traditions' shared optimism about the efficacy of moral education, self-cultivation, and social interaction. Such historical-mindedness nurtured a powerful fundamentalist poetics dedicated to aligning literature with public service.

The Way of learning

Though legalism, with its reliance on rules and punishments, held sway during the short-lived Qin dynasty (221–207 BCE), during the long Han dynasty (206 BCE–220 CE) traditionalist thinkers turned to classical texts to learn from historical precedent the best ways to cultivate moral behavior. Like many texts compiled during the Han, the *Record of Ritual* 禮記 makes explicit morality's dependence on learning. In it, Confucius links deep study of the classics with the habituation of virtues:

> When people are warm, gentle, and guileless,
> surely they have been taught the *Classic of Poetry*.

The passage goes on to link broad-mindedness with the study of history, generosity with the study of music, and honesty with philosophy:

When people are pure and quiet, refined yet humble,
surely they have been taught the *Classic of Changes*.

In its efforts to legitimate its imperial rule, the Han
promoted traditionalist learning by codifying the classics and
institutionalizing a synthesis of Confucian, Daoist, and naturalist
thought. Han scholars argued for a moral basis to the five-agents
correspondences whereby, as Confucius taught, moral conduct
follows heaven's will. Seeing natural changes as transformations of
qi, these thinkers saw regulating one's *qi* as integral to developing
intuition and wisdom. While Daoists offered other techniques,
traditionalist scholars made studying texts an important method
for refining one's *qi*.

Although Daoism, Buddhism, and other schools of thought were
as influential as Confucianism from the collapse of the Han
through the period of disunion and the Tang dynasty, traditionalist
learning was restored to a central place during the Song dynasty
(960–1279). For though the Song reunified China and reestablished
a centralized bureaucracy for the first time since the devastating
An Lushan rebellion (755–63), the dynasty never sought the Tang's
military power or geographical reach. Since warlords had brought
down the Tang, Song emperors sought to privilege civil rule
above military might. To this end, they recruited officials through
an expanded examination system based on mastery of classical
Confucian texts. This system raised the power of literary culture to
unprecedented heights and fostered a gentry class of elite families
whose prestige depended on literary education and office holding.

During the Song, watershed political, social, and economic
changes led to new understandings of literary culture. With its
flourishing cities, the largest and most advanced in the world, Song
culture included a hitherto unknown variety of new occupations,
manufactured products, and popular entertainments. During
the "Northern Song" (when the capital was in the northern
commercial center of Kaifeng), a commitment to literary culture

required a commitment to service and vice versa. Yet after invaders conquered northern China in 1126, the Song lived under constant threats of war, and by the late "Southern Song" many thinkers turned to reworking Confucian thought into a more personal moral philosophy.

Seeking certainty in traditionalist texts, a school of "Way Learning" 道學 developed to establish a source of authority among the many conflicting schools of thought. Also known as "Principle Learning" 理學, and called Neo-Confucianism in English, this school's most important philosopher was Zhu Xi 朱熹 (1130–1200). Making rational principle (*li* 理) the foundation, Zhu boldly combined his predecessors' disparate theories into a creative synthesis.

Though Zhu himself suffered political disgrace, after his death his synthesis would become orthodoxy for more than half a millennium. According to his philosophy, people were born with the goodness of principle, but their material energy (*qi*), subject as it was to chance, could become muddy. To realign one's mind with natural principle, Zhu Xi recommended "quiet sitting" and the "investigation of things." Furthering traditional optimism about the efficacy of moral education, neo-Confucian thinkers thus relied more than ever on self-cultivation through textual study.

Though the idealist neo-Confucian philosopher Wang Yangming 王陽明 (1472–1529) later argued against Zhu Xi's emphasis on rational knowledge in favor of intuitive knowledge inseparable from action, Zhu Xi's emphasis on study of the Confucian classics continued to dominate elite education and the recruitment of officials. After the invading Mongols established the Yuan dynasty (1279–1368), their discontinuation of the civil service examinations briefly left the literati without a unified educational curriculum. Yet from the reinstatement of the exam system in 1313 until its abolition in 1905, all candidates studied Zhu Xi's commentaries on the "Four Books" he selected as the core neo-Confucian canon: the *Analects*, the *Mencius*, the *Great Learning* 大學, and the *Central Mean* 中庸.

After overcoming Mongol rule, the governing elite of the Chinese Ming dynasty (1368–1644) took even more seriously their responsibility to educate younger men in the textual patrimony. To bolster cultural unity, the Ming reconstructed a common orthodoxy based in the neo-Confucian tradition, and this orthodoxy endured even after the northern Manchus established the Qing dynasty (1644–1911). Anxious about their legitimacy, the Qing rulers were even more concerned about orthodoxy, and their examinations required candidates to write a particularly rule-bound "eight-legged essay" rather than poetry. Qing scholars also reinforced the rationalist tradition by developing methods of evidential research and by producing gigantic dictionaries, anthologies, and encyclopedias. With the *Complete Library of the Four Treasuries* 四庫全書 (1773–82), a huge compendium of 3,461 works accompanied by an extensive annotated bibliography, the Manchus appropriated the Chinese textual tradition, co-opted Han scholars as compilers, and, by controlling and preserving permissible texts, marginalized works that might threaten their rule. This compilation, which excluded plays and novels, profoundly influenced the legacy of pre-modern Chinese literature.

The Way of nature

The foundations of an alternative literary aesthetic can be found in the earliest texts later classified as Daoist. These texts present nature as a potter's wheel molding the "ten thousand things" according to its Way (*Dao* 道), the holistic path of eternal generation and decay. The foundational text of this tradition is the *Laozi* 老子, better known in the West as the *Daodejing* 道德經. Probably compiled in the third century BCE, this collection records the teachings of the Old Master(s) 老子 (ca. sixth century BCE). The foundation for almost every lineage of Daoist philosophical and religious schools, these elusive sayings celebrate yielding to the flow of what is (*ziran* 自然, lit., "the self so" and later the term for "nature").

Seventy-Six

When born, people are gentle and feeble;
When dead, they become unyielding and tough.
Living, ten thousand creatures and plants are pliant and crisp;
When dead, they become withered and parched.
Thus the unyielding and tough are death's apprentices;
The gentle and feeble are apprentices of life.
A military reliant on toughness will not triumph;
A tree too tough will be broken.
The tough and great dwell down below;
The gentle and feeble dwell above.

Deeply distrustful of the imposition of names and categories, the *Laozi* celebrates intuitive apprehension. Seeing all forms of coercion and grasping, including mental abstractions, as misleading people from the Way, the text encourages an appreciation of emptiness. Just as it is the space in a bowl that makes it useful, it is often the empty space in a painting that makes it beautiful, and the spontaneous movements that create a dance. Such esteem for effortless action and for negative space would have a profound influence on Chinese poetry and painting.

The second foundational Daoist text, the *Zhuangzi* 莊子, offers parables directly critiquing coercive effort. In one, a young man journeys to Handan because he admires the Handanites' gait. He mimics them but cannot learn, and in trying he forgets his own way of walking and has to crawl home. Full of such satirical anecdotes, lyrical allegories, puns, and word plays, the *Zhuangzi* may be China's earliest fictional work. A composite probably compiled in the fourth century CE, its first seven "Inner Chapters" may have been written by the skeptical nonconformist Zhuang Zhou 莊周 (ca. 369–286 BCE). Unlike

Confucius, who longed for political influence but accepted his role as a teacher, Zhuangzi had no taste for politics. When asked to become an administrator, he declined by asking the envoys a simple question: Would they prefer to be a preserved tortoise venerated in a temple or a live tortoise lugging its tail in the mud?

Keenly aware of the great diversity of the "ten thousand things" (including creatures), Zhuangzi was acutely critical of preconceptions, morals, laws, and institutions that impose uniformity. Seeing only convention as accounting for the naming of objects, Zhuangzi opposed the moral precepts of traditionalist scholars. Rather than using words to conceptualize, categorize, and artificially differentiate between right and wrong, benefit and harm, self and others, the *Zhuangzi* encourages attending to an undifferentiated whole.

Zhuangzi's humility before the world of phenomena led to his deep trust in wandering. Through free spontaneous movement one could become attuned to the natural Way and respond with sensitivity and equanimity to natural tendencies. By cultivating such attentiveness in lieu of deliberate control, one could ride the chariot of the six energies of *yin* and *yang*, wind and rain, dark and light. To Zhuangzi, the operations of emotions, from rage to joy to recklessness, were but "mushrooms forming in ground mist." Of unknowable provenance, their flow might or might not be in anyone's control. "Without them there is no me, and without me they have nothing to hold on to." And yet Zhuangzi found joy whenever he could, as in his insistence that the fish are happy in his famous conversation above the Hao River. By highlighting the relativity of judgments, this parable conveys the role of language and communication not only in creating knowledge and points of view but in giving rise to happiness and other emotions.

Thousands of rewritings testify to the profound influence of Zhuangzi's parables and other Daoist allusions. In "Old Air Nine"

古風其九, for example, the poet Li Bai 李白 (701-62) invokes
Zhuangzi to dispute the value of conventional worldly pursuits.

> Zhuang Zhou dreamt of a butterfly,
> The butterfly then became Zhuang Zhou.
> A body continually changes,
> Ten thousand things in nature's tow.
> The vast Penglai waters you now know
> Will return to a clear and shallow flow.
> The Green Gate melon grower
> Was Count of Dong-ling long ago.
> Since wealth and status pass so,
> Why this restless seeking to and fro?

Zhuangzi's emphasis on nurturing life offered an important
alternative to traditionalist poetics that made it literature's
purpose to better the state. Against the traditionalists' emphasis
on effort and book learning, the *Zhuangzi* celebrates the wisdom
of experience. Praising a cicada catcher, a woodcarver, and a
swimmer, among others, Zhuangzi most memorably celebrates
a cook who uses his spirit rather than his eyes to cut up a steer.
Effortlessly wielding his blade through natural cavities, never
hacking, he sharpens his knife only after nineteen years. In the
Zhuangzi, such easy mastery through practice fares far better than
reading the ancients. As a wheelwright tells a studious duke, since
the ancients have died and a skill such as cutting a wheel cannot be
told in words, what he is reading is "nothing more than the dregs
of the ancients."

Emphasis on nature gained influence after the collapse of the Han
dynasty (206 BCE–220 CE) led to serious questioning of Confucian
doctrines and system building. Turning away from writing devoted
to public service toward quests for personal and spiritual meaning,
works such as Ji Kang's 嵇康 (223–62) essay "Nourishing Life"
養生論 and Ge Hong's 葛洪 (284–364) *The Master Who Cherishes
Simplicity* 抱朴子 introduced methods for pursuing immortality,

and a school of "profound learning" developed out of reflections on the *Classic of Changes*, the *Laozi*, and the *Zhuangzi*. Dedicated to this form of mysticism, thinkers sought union with the Way through contemplating nature. For a scholar-official alienated from political influence, nature provided a home, a framework, and an expansive view beyond worldly frustrations. The cultivation of this wider view also conferred a sense of worth on the connoisseur. By contemplating mountains and rivers, rocks and streams, one could understand the balance of movement and quiet and, through writing, manifest both the natural order and one's own cultivated virtue.

The Way of feeling

Seeking the Way also meant confronting the powerful role of emotions and desires. The term *qing* 情 came to mean emotions and passion only during the Han dynasty; the word originally referred to genuineness. This notion of genuineness informed early debates about whether goodness originated in human nature or had to be developed through moral education. In recounting landmarks of his life, Confucius noted that at seventy he could follow the desires of his heart without transgressing moral principles. If the heart is aligned, this avowal implies, one's desires will guide one to moral action. With faith in the four innate tendencies of compassion, shame, modesty, and a sense of right and wrong, Mencius valued feelings as noble sentiments grounded in genuine yearnings for goodness. According to Mencius, by nurturing vital *qi*, courage, and temperament, one could strengthen moral intentions, avoid distraction from the heart-mind, and achieve resonance with the universe. Though less sanguine about human nature, Xunzi also recommended controlling passions for good ends. Nurturing desires and feelings thus became one of literary culture's key functions.

As poetry and other forms of writing developed as important means of expressing and regulating emotions, attention to subtle moods became a staple of poetic theory. Growing esteem for emotion is voiced in the first systematic work of literary theory, Liu Xie's 劉勰 fifth-century *Writing the Heart-mind, Carving the Dragon* 文心雕龍: "People are endowed with seven emotions. Responding to things of the world these emotions are moved. So moved by things, they sing aspirations; none of this is unnatural." Such positive views of emotions have remained an important stream of Chinese thought, and Liu's text is just one in a tradition that viewed feelings as heavenly dispositions fundamental to inspiration, nurturing *qi*, and the balance of "wind and bone," continuity and transformation, and the hidden and manifest. If literature was "written in the stars," as Liu Xie claimed, it was because the heart-mind could be aligned with heaven's will.

Yet early texts also express concerns about regulating resentment and other negative emotions. The *Record of Ritual* warns of becoming a slave to desires, and its most famous chapter, "The Great Learning," presents anger, terror, worry, and other passions as obstacles to rectifying the mind in accordance with heavenly principles. By the Han dynasty, thinkers began to associate the goodness of original human nature with *yang* and the cloudy nature of the emotions with *yin*. This distinction gained currency as later thinkers likened the mind to water, its ground of calm granted by natural principle but disturbed by the flow of emotions and waves of desire.

Concerns about emotions disordering the mind increased with the spread of Buddhism. The Buddha's teachings of the Four Noble Truths counseled a wariness of the wages of desire. Life is filled with suffering, and suffering is caused by desire; teach the first two truths, and to lessen suffering one must eliminate desire, adds the third. The fourth outlines an eightfold path, where "right intention" includes a commitment to resisting desire, anger, and aversion.

Yet while passions and desires may be primary causes of accumulated *karma,* emotion was also seen as a path to enlightenment. During the medieval period (from the Han through the Tang dynasties), thinkers influenced by Daoism advocated abandoning traditionalist norms and rites. Blaming these rites for spoiling the genuineness of human nature, they encouraged following the organic cycles of the natural world. Paradoxically, this union with natural principle also meant liberation from individual personality and personal desires. Such paradoxes would become major themes of poems, stories, plays, and novels. In the ninth-century tale "Du Zichun" 杜子春, for example, the protagonist of the title forfeits his chance to achieve immortality when, after swallowing three pills to embark on a spiritual journey, he ultimately breaks his Daoist benefactor's injunction against speaking. He manages to free himself from desires and aversions throughout many trials, but when incarnated as a woman whose husband kills their baby out of frustration over her silence, (s)he succumbs to love and cries out "No."

Over time more and more works explicitly endorsed using feeling to awaken to the Way. Seen as the source of aesthetic, imaginative, and subjective consciousness, the term *qing* came to encompass not only all the richness of the English word *love* but also affection, emotions, and sentience. Poetry, fiction, and drama all valorized feeling, and tended to portray emotion rather than rational principle as the driving energy of human affairs. As many traditionalist thinkers came to view feeling as vital to fostering Confucian virtues, feeling was elevated to a cultural and national ideal. This expanded interest in feeling stressed both romantic love and loyalty to the state and emperor, an emphasis that encouraged martyrdom among Chinese literati in the face of the Manchus' conquest and rule. These shifting notions of *qing* suggest feeling's centrality to understandings of how people relate to the world, understandings developed above all in poetry, China's most revered literary genre.

Chapter 2
Poetry and poetics: landscapes, allusions, and alcohol

Dwelling poetically

In "Reed Bank and Fishing Boat" 蘆灘釣艇圖, Wu Zhen's 吳鎮 (1280–1354) poem occupies more space than the fisherman subject, albeit less than the bank of reeds that frames the water on which both float. As the calligraphy, the painting, and the poem's meaning form an integrated whole, the hand scroll serves as a microcosm of the larger natural world and its inherent patterns.

> Fading sunlight lingers on red leaves west of town.
> First traces of moon reveal yellow reeds upon the shore.
> Feathering his oar, to return once more,
> He hangs up his pole, the fish for now ignored.

Reflecting on the play of light and shadow, the fisherman sees beyond his labor, and the reader may sense in the fisherman's respite-taking a range of emotions, from serenity through acceptance to unease and even brooding, and then maybe back again. For the fisherman could also symbolize the unemployed scholar, a particularly poignant theme among disenfranchised literati under the Mongols' Yuan dynasty. Like the waves on the water or the reeds in the wind, this fluctuation of feeling catalyzes the work's emotional power. Often called "silent poems," paintings could convey feelings not easily put into words; calligraphy was thought to be a window on

5. One of the Four Great Masters of the late Yuan dynasty, Wu Zhen integrated calligraphy, poetry, and painting in his "Fisherman," also known as "Reed Bank and Fishing Boat" (ca. 1350).

personality; and poems were charged with evoking nature's manifold mysteries in all their emotional and historical resonance.

In China, poetry has long served a broad range of purposes, from cultivating the self to promoting social harmony to ordering the world. Seen as manifesting nature's patterns, poetry offered ways to find meaning amid time's transience, regulate bodily energies, and cultivate benevolence. "Poetry derives from emotion in patterned

splendor," wrote Lu Ji 陸機 (261–303) in his "Rhyme-prose on Literature" 文賦, and poetry's power to express complex feelings made its composition well suited for both solitary reflection and social gatherings. Often written to commemorate special occasions, many poems note the time, place, and circumstances, either in the title or in a preface. Exchanging such poetry helped document and deepen relationships and fostered political stability.

These diverse functions made poetry one of the most highly esteemed forms of writing in traditional China. Ancient regimes collected folk songs; classics, histories, philosophy texts, and anthologies all included poems. By the third century, elite patronage allowed scholars to devote themselves to poetry, and writing poetry was virtually required of the scholar class. In the late seventh century, the Tang court institutionalized this requirement by including the composition of rhapsodies and poems on the unified civil-service examinations. Although some modern scholars dismiss poetry after the Tang as primarily imitation, throughout the imperial period itself poetry continued to be the most highly esteemed literary genre.

Poetry's power often depends on appealing to energies that elude the rational mind, and Chinese poetry excels in its subtle moods and shifting feelings. In the "Twenty-Four Categories of Poetry" 二十四詩品, for example, the poet-critic Sikong Tu 司空圖 (837–908) not only addresses feelings such as melancholy and "expansive contentment" but juxtaposes dynamic moods, such as "essence and spirit," with more static moods such as "close-woven and dense." Sikong's treatise, itself a long lyrical poem that might as easily describe aspects of personality as poetry, begins with a poem on "potent chaos," then balances it with verses on "limpid and calm," which reflect on the quality's elusiveness.

> Encounter it, for it is not deeply hidden.
> But approach it, and it makes itself more scarce.
> It slips away from any semblance of shape,
> For the grasping hand has already violated it.

Some of these moods, or "modes," focus on the human world ("decorous and elegant"); others point to what lies beyond human conventions ("transcendence," "drifting above it all"). And whereas categories of "the natural" and "the solid world" focus on concrete appearances, modes such as "reserve and accumulation" and "flowing movement" privilege intangible metamorphoses. Frequently overlapping, these poetic modes evoke rich interwoven dimensions of Chinese poetry. A single landscape poem, for example, might offer not only a path beyond the world of "red dust" ("drifting above it all") but also an intimacy with natural surroundings and one's own heart ("limpid and calm").

The solid world

From the earliest poems, reflections on humanity's place in nature fostered lyrical responses to the solid world, and awareness of transience led to a vital *carpe diem* or "seize the day" response. Pleasure, however transient, is accorded an important place in the *Classic of Poetry* 詩經 (1100–600 BCE), the world's earliest example of rhymed verse. Alongside poems that attest to the importance of ritual or commemorate dynastic conquest, other poems celebrate the simple pleasures of carnal love and show a keen awareness of the passage of time. The brevity of human life makes it all the more important to enjoy the present, suggests "Crickets" 蟋蟀, whose second stanza begins,

> The crickets are in the hall;
> The years and months pass on.
> If we do not rejoice today
> The sun and moons will run on.

Such songs express exuberance in living according to nature's patterns and enjoying simple activities of courtship, marriage, farming, dancing, and feasting. Many also urge people not to waste life's precious moments striving for glory or trying too hard to understand human affairs. Health is more important than achievement, proclaims "Don't Push Onward the Great Carriage" 無將大車:

> Don't push onward the great carriage,
> You will just make yourself dusty.
> Don't think of a hundred worries,
> You will just make yourself sick.

29

As poems connect human life to seasonal patterns, discrepancies between societal expectations and seasonal markers provoke painful anxiety. In "The Gourd Has Bitter Leaves" 匏有苦葉, for example, a young woman despairs that her future husband has not come for her before the ice melts, as is the custom. This oblique but lyrical method of projecting joys, fears, and other feelings through images from the natural world (called "pathetic fallacy" in literary rhetoric) would become prevalent in all the literary traditions of East Asia.

Legend has it that officials roamed the realm to gather the 305 airs, ballads, odes, and hymns of the *Classic of Poetry*. Whether really of popular origin or written for the court, the odes were likely originally sung, and this oral tradition may account for their generous use of repetition, onomatopoeia, and other formulas popular among professional singers. Though it continued to evolve, the book took its basic shape about 600 BCE and, as the earliest anthology of Chinese poetry, serves as both a foundation of the literary tradition and a key source of information about ancient Chinese culture.

From the earliest commentaries, scholars drew moral lessons from these poems, and this subordination of literature to didactic purposes set a powerful precedent. The claim that Confucius had edited the poems prompted conjecture about their moral and historical significance, and these allegorical interpretations, often politically motivated, held sway until the Song dynasty. The influential "Great Preface" 大序, added in the first century CE, developed Confucius's views on poetry by expanding on the idea that "Poetry expresses intent," a line from the ancient *Classic of Documents*. Because "intent" could refer to involuntary feelings but also to moral ambition, this definition charged poetry with conveying the moral Way. Commenting on the "Great Preface," the Confucian scholar Kong Yingda 孔穎達 (574–648) expanded on this idea to clarify the shared genesis of feelings and moral intentions: "When emotions are moved, they become intentions. Emotions and intentions are indeed one."

Seizing the day also meant celebrating the natural world, and the "Great Preface" introduces a mode of discourse unique to Chinese poetics for responding to external stimuli. Whereas exposition (*fu* 賦) describes and analogy (*bi* 比) compares, the evocative "incitement" (*xing* 興) serves as a catalyst for an emotional response. The *xing* often opens a poem to announce the dominant image—as in such first lines as "Look at the rat, it has its skin," "Soaking is the dew," and "Swampland mulberries are lovely," and the *xing* image or sound often repeats as a refrain to set the mood, rhythm, or sound pattern. In contrast to the emphasis on mimesis in much Western poetry, this recording of natural stimuli suggests that the poems were a direct reaction to, rather than an imitation of, the world. In contrast to the notion of a poet transmitting an individual subjective experience to readers, the term honors poetry as a vessel for shared emotion. (As with much Chinese literary terminology, emphasis on emotional effect overshadows concerns with distinct formal features.)

Focus on the here and now would remain a dominant mode of later poetry. Many accounts of simple pleasures subtly expressed dissent against exploitation and were an important means by which China's long tradition of antiwar poetry addressed the costs of empire building. In Wang Han's 王翰 (687–726) quatrain "Song of Liangzhou" 涼州詞, for example, a despairing soldier justifies his drunkenness by invoking the countless unknown dead.

> For fine wine in gleaming cups at night we yearned,
> Even as the martial pluck-pluck urged us back up in turn.
> If we lie drunk on the battlefield, don't laugh, my lord,
> Of all to fight since ancient times, how many have returned?

Transcendence

In contrast to the more rational tradition, often associated with the north and initiated by a focus on the solid world in the *Classic of Poetry*, a mystical southern tradition of poetry flourished in the region around the Yangtze River in the ancient southern state of Chu (seventh to third centuries BCE). *The Elegies of Chu* 楚辭, the extant collection of this poetry, recalls a vibrant culture of shaman mediums, healers who addressed and even embodied nature deities. Full of appeals to the god of the clouds, the god of the Yellow River, and two sister goddesses of the Xiang River, the *Elegies*, by privileging female spirits and shamanesses, departed from the dominant tradition's subordination of women. Whereas much of older poetry, including the *Classic of Poetry*, used four-character lines, the *Elegies*' longer lines allowed for more narration. Though never a canonical "classic," this collection won esteem thanks to a second-century edition presented in the high commentary tradition that accorded prestige.

Encountering Sorrow 離騷, the most famous work of the *Elegies*, is a long narrative poem by China's earliest named poet, the Chu statesman Qu Yuan 屈原 (340–278 BCE). As Qu's speaker repeatedly alludes to time's swift passage and the fading of youth, the pressure he feels to achieve greatness contrasts sharply with the appreciation of simple pleasures in the *Classic of Poetry*. Unjustly slandered and banished, Qu Yuan feared that his loyalty would be squandered, and the 187 couplets of his elegy depict a decadent age of a world upside down, in which the virtuous fall yet the corrupt prosper.

Read primarily as an epic of political protest, *Encountering Sorrow* established enduring conventions for expressing defiance. Together with odes from the *Classic of Poetry*, *Encountering Sorrow* is the *locus classicus* of the image of a neglected lover as a metaphor for a statesman unappreciated by his ruler. The first part of the poem describes in fairly realistic terms the speaker's failure to meet with the good graces of his beloved. Fearing his beloved's beauty to be withering, and seeing all around him as corrupt and muddied, the speaker resolves to make a journey to find someone who can understand his heart.

> Long long is my road and far far my journey;
> I will travel up and down, searching.

The poem then depicts the speaker's desperate effort to challenge his fate in a mystical journey through celestial realms. As if trying to outrun the sunset, he heads ever westward. In the end, after the gatekeeper of heaven only laughs at him, and nowhere within his kingdom can he find a worthy partner, a shaman advises him to seek beyond the Chu state. He resolves to take his search elsewhere, a choice that could suggest either spiritual transcendence or a renunciation of his country for unknown lands. Just as he is about to achieve transcendence, he falters.

> Just as I climbed the exalted luminous heights,
> Unexpectedly I glanced down and saw my old home.
> My driver, saddened, and my horses, their hearts swelling,
> Craned back their necks to look and would not go on.

His devotion to his home, and thereby to his human condition and sentimental attachments, is too strong, and his valiant challenge of his limited destiny proves futile. Frustrated, the speaker resolves to follow the example of worthy ancients who drowned themselves.

According to legend, Qu Yuan drowned himself in the Miluo River, and his elegy has been read autobiographically. These interpretations underpin a long tradition wherein Chinese scholars have used biographical information to explain texts and used texts to construct biographies of their authors. Though circular, this method of biographical inference underscores literature's relevance. Modern critics might decry such wide recourse to the "intentional fallacy," but the habit of viewing a poem's speaker as the poet him- or herself also reveals the tradition's keen awareness that a poem is a dramatic event, a speaker's response to a specific situation. Beginning with the martyr Qu Yuan, poems were among the first texts in which individual speakers expressed themselves and their desires, and thereby claimed the authority to remonstrate.

Decorous and elegant

In the face of political upheavals and natural disasters, poetry's ordered elegance offered solace. And amid historical contingencies and fluctuations of feelings, the persistence of certain genres, themes, and images testifies to the comfort of familiar forms. Whether poets followed conventions of occasional poetry, eremitic traditions devoted to nature, or more socially engaged traditions, they often used rewriting practices that were decidedly not in pursuit of originality.

In one major line of development, the southern tradition of Qu's *Encountering Sorrow* nurtured the development of rhapsodies (*fu* 賦). Most Chinese poetry is more suggestive than exhaustive, but during the Han dynasty (206 BCE–220 CE), when system building was paramount, these detailed expositions in verse became the dominant poetic genre. Also known as "rhyme-prose" because some *fu* are closer to essays written in a mixture of prose and verse, the term *fu* originally meant "to lay out" or "to unfold," and early rhapsodies presented elaborate descriptive lists of flora, fauna, majestic parks, and grand cities.

Longer rhapsodies describe hunting parks and capital cities, while shorter rhapsodies often present nightmares, zithers, owls, orangutans, and caged birds, often symbolic of an able but confined scholar. Reinforcing faith in cosmic patterns (*wen* 文), writers frequently patterned their rhapsodies according to the categories in correlative cosmology. In the opening lines of Mi Heng's 禰衡 (ca. 173–98) "Rhapsody on a Parrot" 鸚鵡賦, for example, the bird's origins, physical appearance, and essential nature follow the system of correspondences insofar as metal (the bird's essence) corresponds to the west (its home) and to white (its color), while fire (its potential) corresponds to red and to the south (perhaps its destination before being captured).

From the Western domain a smart bird so divine,
It projects the rare beauty of nature so fine.
Embodying the mystical substance of metal quintessence,
It contains the power of fire's bright luminescence.
By nature wise and discerning, it thus can converse
Using astute talent to recognize the motions of the universe.

Following the conventions of court "rhapsodies on objects"
詠物賦, after an opening treatment of the bird's exotic origins and
their cosmological associations, the rhapsody offers an account
of the bird's capture tactful enough not to ruin the pleasure of the
text. It then describes the bird's life in captivity, and ends with a
section declaring the bird's gratitude and devotion to its master.
Yet rather than restrain his vocabulary to discrete euphemisms,
Mi Heng explicitly describes the parrot's form as "mournful and
wasted," inspiring those who hear it to grieve and those who see
it to weep. Poignant lines near the end make clear that, however
fervently the parrot longs for home, his masters have maimed its
wings beyond hope:

Dreaming of the high peaks of Kunlun,
Longing for the dense verdure of the Forest of Deng.
But then it thinks of its mutilated wings;
Flap as it may, where will they take it?

Such lines belie the closing section's presentation of the parrot's
supposed desire to serve and repay its master. The rhapsody had
already expressed veiled criticism in the middle section by asking
whether the bird's hard fate "is because speech leads to disaster, or
telling secrets puts one in danger." The inference that corruption
marks the official world suggests the subtle narrative power of
rhapsodic metaphor.

Although the ornamentation of rhapsodies was derided as mere
"insect carving" by those committed to identifying written words
with the moral heart of the writer, rhapsodies remained the

most respected form of verse throughout the medieval period (through the ninth century). Statesmen excelled at the elegant genre, as can be seen in Cao Zhi's 曹植 (192–232) "Rhapsody on the Luo River Goddess" 洛神賦. Cao's worshipful description turns somber when the speaker's doubts trouble the goddess. Sympathetic to her disappointment, the wind god stops blowing, the water goddess halts the waves, and a contingent of goddesses, dragons, and waterfowl accompany the river goddess back to the heavens. Though scholars dispute later interpreters' reading of Cao's rhapsody as a veiled testimony to his love for his brother's wife the empress, the power of these combined mythical and historical legends inspired numerous later poems, tales, and operas.

Melancholy and regret

In contrast to the constructivist mode of rhapsodies, a more expressive mode marks China's long tradition of folk ballads and lyrical poetry (*shi* 詩). During the Han dynasty, the court delegated the management of music and poetry to the Music Bureau, an institution that employed more than nine hundred workers. Collecting poems and music from within and beyond the empire, these officials combined existing motifs and structures with new meters. By the turn of the millennium, musical trends led to the dominance of the five-character line, early examples of which figure among the highlights of world literature.

The earliest extant collection of pentasyllabic poems is the *Nineteen Old Poems* 古詩十九首 from the end of the Later Han (25–220). Seemingly straightforward, several of these poems recount military expeditions, but the second poem expresses a woman's lament of her solitude. Like many Chinese poems, the poem begins with a scenic description and then unveils the subject's emotions.

Green green, river bank grasses,
thick thick, willows in the garden;
plump plump, the lady in the tower,
bright bright, before the window;
lovely lovely, her red face-powder;
slim slim, she puts out a white hand.
Once a singing-house girl,
now the wife of a wanderer,
a wanderer who never comes home —
It's hard sleeping in an empty bed alone.

In the first six lines, a scenic description of spring gradually closes in on the forlorn subject. The river borders a forest, which surrounds a tower, whose windows frame a lonely woman. From the natural to the manmade world, the layers of description move step by step into her chamber, where her confinement heightens the pathos of her delicate gesture. Bound inside, she can only stretch out her hand.

The final four lines shift to an account of the woman's past and current predicament. She is the wife of a "wayward wanderer," a term connoting that she has been deserted. But were her husband not a wanderer, would he have married a lowly singing girl? Although the opening describes the woman as a static object, here the poem shifts to her perspective. (Since the original, like most classical Chinese poems, uses no pronouns, the subject may or may not be the speaker.) As she sees the empty bed, she almost sees herself by the bedside. Only the very last line voices her loneliness, but the opening's simple objective description builds up this line's power. The beginning, it turns out, presented a façade through which the pathos of this last line breaks. Though seductively beautiful, each layer of description further binds the woman, and the continuation of the natural cycle accentuates her fixed isolation. In contrast to the natural world's dynamic movement, she is static and quiet.

Or is she? Some read the last line as suggesting a longing for a tryst, an interpretation more evident in Stephen Owen's translation: "A lonely bed can't be kept empty for long." Such ambiguity reminds us that movement and quiet are always in tension, and that when a situation reaches an extreme, it will often reverse toward the other pole.

This theme of the neglected woman, often a symbol of life's transience, gained prominence in the medieval period and thereafter. Even though most surviving poems were written by men, they frequently adopt a female persona as a metaphor for the neglected loyal minister, and in time poems on neglected palace women formed a major subgenre. The elegance of such poems can be seen in Xie Tiao's 謝朓 (464–99) "Jade Steps Lament" 玉階怨, one of five hundred "palace style poems" collected in the sixth-century anthology *New Songs from a Jade Terrace* 玉臺新詠.

> In the evening palace I lower the pearl screen,
> Aimless fireflies soar about, then poise, then soar again.
> In the long night I sew silk garments, longing for you,
> This anguish must end, but when?

In a poem by the same title, Li Bai 李白 (701–62), one of China's two most acclaimed poets, recasts Xie Tiao's treatment:

> On the jade steps forms white dew,
> After a long time at night the dew invades my stockings.
> Returning to lower the crystal curtain,
> Through the transparent screen I gaze at the autumn moon.

The subtle upward movement of the visual focus (from steps, to feet, to curtain, to moon) helps explain this poem's place among celebrated masterpieces. Such a ranking was in no way diminished when a poem was a rewriting. Reworking dominant themes such as remonstrance and defiance, the neglected lover, and time's transience allowed poets to focus on technique, and copious allusions heightened appreciation. As the calligrapher-poet-painter Huang Tingjian 黃庭堅 (1045–1105) wrote of earlier masters, "though taking the ancients' set expressions into their writing brushes and ink, as if with a particle of cinnabar, [they] transmuted iron into gold." This image of Daoist alchemy captures well poets' efforts to reanimate words used earlier to evoke a sympathetic resonance in like-minded listeners.

With the evolution of musical entertainment, the culture of romance, languor, and longing further developed with the lyric (*ci* 詞), another major genre of Chinese poetry. From the eighth century on, these song texts were written to melodies, including tunes from Central Asia that required different line lengths from those used in *shi* 詩 poetry. Allowing for more flexibility in the numbers of characters per line, these lyrics centered on scenic descriptions, send-off poems, longing for absent friends, melancholy, nostalgia, historical vicissitudes, eulogies to beautiful women, and, most of all, the plaints of neglected women, frequently allegories for unappreciated ministers.

Often performed by courtesans, some of these lyrics used more vernacular diction, and serious writers took pains to distinguish their elegant lyrics from more common ones. Yet elite women also wrote lyrics, and China's most famous woman poet, Li Qingzhao 李清照 (1084–1151) is one of the genre's most accomplished practitioners. With access to books in her husband's private library, Li enjoyed uncommon privilege until Jurchen invaders conquered the north and forced her to flee south. After her husband died of malaria, her lyrics and poems reached heights of poignancy. In "To the Tune of 'Wuling Spring'" 武陵春, the speaker laments, "Now he is no more," and the lyric's second half confronts her burden of grief:

> I dream of floating in a light boat at Twin-stream,
>> which they say retains the bloom of spring.
> Only my boat, tiny as a grasshopper, couldn't bear, I fear,
>> the load of grief I'd bring.

Separation and rusticity

Because visible aspects of the everyday world were seen as
manifestations of the Way, images of concrete scenery could also
serve as a limpid mirror for the expression of intangible feeling.
Unlike romantic conceptions of "inner" feelings, Chinese poems
tend to present feelings as coming alive through interpersonal
exchanges in concrete situations. The pleasures of good company
became an especially frequent theme in the medieval period as

6. Literati have long treasured bamboo as a symbol of loyalty,
steadfastness, and integrity. The bamboo's "empty heart" has also made
it a symbol of modesty and an esteemed art motif, as in this fourteenth-
century painting by Ni Zan 倪瓚.

social groups formed, such as the "Seven Sages of the Bamboo Grove." This group of eccentric literati purportedly met on the estate of Ji Kang 嵇康 (223–62) to drink, enjoy the landscape, write poetry, and engage in "pure conversation." Wishing to escape political entanglements, these poets celebrated simple rustic life, and their hedonistic pleasures have been much speculated upon.

The group's most important poet was Ruan Ji 阮籍 (210–63), whose eighty-two poems *Singing My Feelings* 詠懷詩 privileged emotion coupled with philosophical reflection. In the sixth of these poems, Ruan celebrates an ancient count who turned to raising melons after the fall of the Qin dynasty. Praising the melons' glowing colors, he contrasts the melon farmer with those in official life.

> The grease-filled torch burns itself out,
> Many riches cause harm and peril.
> Cotton clothes can be worn 'til life's end,
> How could we rely on lavish stipends so sterile?

Such contemplative, bucolic poetry could also serve as a means of political protest. Although the Confucian tradition urged rulers to welcome criticism as loyal efforts to ameliorate the state, officials who dared to voice criticism were often demoted and exiled to distant posts. When persuasion or protest was to no avail, a person of virtue could withdraw into nature. Thus a good Confucian official could become a recluse (隱士, lit., a "hiding scholar") and withdraw from the worldly pursuit of fame, wealth, and power.

Celebrations of nature and feeling did not reconcile the dilemma between struggling for worldly achievements and finding solace in simple pleasures. Conflicting desires for participation in society and retreat into nature mark many poems of Tao Qian 陶潛 (365–427), a poet whose oeuvre was created as much by editors as by Tao himself. Tao's reputation—not highly esteemed during his lifetime—was established by Song-dynasty neo-Confucian scholars who appreciated his poems' relative freedom from Buddhist influence. Thanks to their promotion, Tao, also known as Tao Yuanming 陶淵明, became the most famous of the "hiding gentlemen" poets and is credited with inventing the "poetry of the fields and gardens" 田園詩, as bucolic poetry came to be known.

Tao's three-poem series "Substance, Shadow, Spirit" 形影神 presents the conflict between worldly ambition and simple pleasures as a debate between different parts of the self. In "Substance Addresses Shadow" 形贈影, substance first laments the inevitability of death's effacement of the individual and then advocates a hedonistic response: "Take my advice, when faced with wine, never say no." In "Shadow Responds to Substance" 影答形, shadow concedes that wine may provide comfort but argues that ease can never compare with doing good and thereby establishing a name that will live on after one dies. Finally, in "Spirit Expounds" 神釋, spirit attempts to resolve the conflict. Pointing out that wine may shorten one's precious life and asking who will remember one after death, spirit advocates accepting fate rather than wearying oneself with worry.

> Too much ruminating injures my life.
> It's better to yield to fate's turns.
> Follow the waves in the great transformation,
> Neither rejoicing nor fearing.
> When all is finished, then end.
> No longer alone so beset with concern.

Spirit's disdain for worldly preoccupations reflects Tao's own views. At the age of thirty-three, after just eighty-three days in office, Tao resigned from official life. "Fettered bird keens for its former woods," he writes of his decision to forsake the "dusty net" of bureaucratic service in his chain of five poems "Returning to Dwell in Gardens and Fields" 歸田園居. With his famous refusal to bow for five bushels of rice, Tao justifies his resignation as a matter of preserving his integrity. Yet his poem series also testifies to the difficulty of escaping from worry. By retreating to his family's small farm, the speaker escapes the confinement of officialdom only to find himself caught in nature's larger web of equally uncontrollable forces. Rising with the dawn to hoe his fields and returning with the moon, the speaker delights in his harmonious place in nature. But he also frets over his precarious existence and the success of his crops. Textual variants intensify debates on whether such poems convey anxiety or calm, and Tao himself famously addressed such paradoxes of communication in the fifth of his twenty poems on "Drinking Alcohol" 飲酒: "A hint of Truth lies within, / But when I want to tell it, I forget the words just as I begin."

Drifting above it all

By the fifth century, as Buddhism encouraged greater attention to the natural world, this influence nurtured a second genre of landscape poetry known as the "poetry of mountains and rivers" 山水詩. This genre was most famously developed by Tao's contemporary Xie Lingyun 謝靈運 (385–433) and by Buddhist-inspired poets such as the painter-poet Wang Wei 王維 (699–761). Wang's poetry was said to contain paintings and his painting said to contain poems, a fusion that can be glimpsed in his quatrain "Deer Fence" 鹿柴.

> No one is seen in deserted hills,
> Only the echoes of speech are heard.
> Sunlight cast back comes deep in the woods
> And shines once again upon the green moss.

By not specifying a subject, Wang may have deliberately sought to express absorption in nature. The first line here is literally 空山不見人 "[In an] empty mountain [I/you/we/she] see(s) no one," and choosing a specific pronoun limits the poem's meaning to one of several overlapping possibilities. The absence of a specific persona is common in classical Chinese poetry, especially landscape poetry, and it is regrettable that translation often requires adding a subject, for the ambiguity could be an artistic response to questions of selfhood. Instead of glorifying an individual subject, Chinese poems often efface the self. Softening the distinction between "subject" and "object," such poems offer reflections on the world less mediated by individual personality.

Contemplative landscape poetry often integrated Chan (禪 "Meditation") Buddhism, a distinctive school developed by Chinese practitioners. Better known abroad by the Japanese pronunciation Zen, Chan teachings turned away from the otherworldly focus of much Indian Buddhism and presented enlightenment as immediately accessible through meditation, simple everyday practices such as flower arranging, and appreciation of the concrete things of daily life.

Alongside Buddhist lay poets such as Wang Wei, Buddhist monk poets such as Wang Fanzhi 王梵志 and Han Shan 寒山 made poetry a means of religious expression. (Rather than an actual person, the persona of Han Shan, literally "Cold Mountain," may have been a device to compile Buddhist lyric poetry.) Although Chan teachings downplay language, literati increasingly likened aesthetic experiences of poetry to awakening in Chan meditation. In *Canglang's Remarks on Poetry* 滄浪詩話, Yan Yu 嚴羽 (ca. 1195–1245) explicitly pursued this approach by identifying five "dharmas" of poetry. In Yan's framework, thanks to formal construction, structural strength, embodiment of *qi*, rousing of excitement, and tone and rhythm, poetry could convey not only the lofty and profound but also qualities such as potent flux, drifting above it all, fortitude in affliction, and bittersweet grief.

Such spiritual concerns marked poetic theory throughout the imperial period. Even scholar-officials primarily devoted to social engagement often wrote and celebrated poetry as a path to enlightenment. One example is the master poet Wang Shizhen 王士禎 (1634–1711), who also served in high offices as president of the Censorate and minister of justice. In his "Remarks on Poetry" 詩話, Wang praised a personal tone of ineffable "spirit resonance," intuition accessed by fusing with the "undifferentiated marvelous" of objective reality.

Moved by the times

Unlike poets who sought refuge in nature or in spiritual enlightenment, Du Fu 杜甫 (712–70), arguably China's greatest poet, was more influenced by Confucian values and sought to write in service to the state. Though frustrated in his official career, Du Fu's poetry provided a sense of collective identity to Tang people. Writing after the An Lushan rebellion (755–63), an uprising in which tens of millions died, Du Fu laments the ruins of his city in "Spring Contemplation."

When Du Fu composed this five-character regulated verse in the spring of 757, An Lushan's Tartar troops had occupied the capital city of Chang'an since December 755. At the time Du Fu's life and poetry centered on the capital region, and the word "nation" in the first line might refer both to the capital and to the whole country. Because the verb "gazing" could also imply hope or longing, the title conveys a hint of regret that might be expressed as "Beholding What Should Be Spring."

Projecting onto nature feelings that might be too painful to experience directly, the poem uses "pathetic fallacy" to lament both the ruin of the capital and the speaker's own declining health. In the first half of the poem, the speaker gazes off at the mountains, then upon the city and its greenery, and finally down at the dew-covered flowers and up at the birds. In the second half, he looks out again at the distant beacon fires, thinks of his family, and notices his own thinning hair. As his gaze alternates from far to near, the visual progression from a hazy distance to clear observation of the tiny drops of dew resonates with the emotional transition from worrying about the nation to worrying about himself and his distant family.

春望
Spring Gazing

國	破	山	河	在
Nation	break	mountains	rivers	exist
城	春	草	木	深
city	spring	grass	trees	deep
感	時	花	濺	淚
feeling	times	flowers	splatter	tears
恨	別	鳥	驚	心
hating	parting	birds	astonished	heart
烽	火	連	三	月
beacon	fires	continue	three	months
家	書	抵	萬	金
family	letter	equivalent	to 10,000	gold
白	頭	搔	更	短
white	head	scratch	even	shorter
渾	欲	不	勝	簪
confused	desire	not	triumph	hairpin

Spring Contemplation

The nation breaks asunder
    while mountains and rivers endure.
The capital faces spring
    overrun by lawless verdure.
Lamenting the times
    the flowers bespatter tears,
Hating separation
    birds alarmed excite my fears.
Blazing beacon fires
    already three months old,
A letter from my family
    would be worth ten thousand gold.
White hair torn at fretfully
    becomes ever more thin,
Soon too sparse
    to hold my cherished hairpin in.

In the first couplet, the constancy of nature alerts the poet to the impermanence of human civilization. As the second line contrasts the exuberance of spring with the devastation of the capital, the thickly overgrown grasses signal the capital's dilapidation. Yet the vegetation might also portend the defeated nation's possible renaissance. To interpret nature's endurance with hope depends on a choice. Whereas the first couplet observes nature's indifference to human sorrows, the second recounts nature's sympathetic grieving. Though not required as in the second and third couplets, the first couplet's grammatical parallelism reinforces this contrast.

The strong pathetic fallacy of the second couplet also lends itself to two interpretations. It could be the poet who is moved to tears and fright by the flowers and birds, or the subject could be the flowers who cry and the birds who take flight, as in "the birds seem startled, as if with the anguish of separation." The ambiguity in these concurrent meanings demonstrates what scholars call "compression" or the "double-grammar" of Chinese poetry. And why, one might ask, would birds scare the poet? It may be because their migration accentuates his stranded condition. By convention, flowers and birds often make people happy, but it is not unusual for Chinese poets to use these elements, especially birds' cries, to express sadness or serve as a foil to the speaker's sorrow.

The third couplet shifts from the contemplation of public disaster to a consideration of personal grief. Routinely used to maintain contact between garrisons, the beacon fires are a symbol of war and thus explain the chaos of the times for which the flowers weep. A state of emergency has existed for three months, line 5 tells us, and just as the words "three months" are parallel to the "10,000 in gold," so the entire third couplet parallels the second as the desire for a letter from home echoes the birds' reluctance to separate.

As the last three lines shift from objective description to subjective reaction, the image of thinning hair is sad but also comic. Without belittling the speaker's distress, the final couplet may convey a change of mood from his earlier anguish to playful self-mockery. Since Du Fu was only forty-five or forty-six in 757, thinning hair might also indicate that the war has aged him prematurely. Might the speaker be tearing out his hair to relieve the angst of helplessness? Such resignation to the futility of efforts against time's fate marked much medieval poetry, especially after the An Lushan rebellion, a war whose death toll was surpassed only by World War II. After the rebellion, the great Tang empire took another century and a half to draw to a close, but in late Tang poetry a sense of the cruel vicissitudes of human endeavors compounded sadness over the brevity of human life.

Heroic abandon

In contrast to Du Fu's world-weariness, other poets embraced a sense of "heroic abandon." Retrospectively, this label can be applied to Du Fu's contemporary Li Bai 李白 (701–62). An eccentric outsider and a practicing Daoist especially loved by nonconformists, Li Bai represents a tradition of Chinese poets who drank quite a bit, sometimes for pleasure and conviviality, and sometimes to break the veil of ordinary consciousness that conceals reality. "Two cups, and I understand the Great Way. / One gallon and I am united with Nature," writes Li Bai in the third poem of his series "Drinking Alone by Moonlight" 月下獨酌.

During the Song era, as fewer literati presumed poetry's connection to a larger order of meaning, debates escalated about the relative importance of poetry's expressive and ethical functions. In contrast to the plaintive refinement of many Tang poems, Song poetry was more supple in structure, more accessible in diction, sometimes even offhand. And by the early twelfth century, literati, especially those who did not seek or receive official appointments, began to form poetry communities. Whereas in earlier periods poets had formed groups, in the Song they formed distinct "schools" (派, lit., "streams"). As fewer and fewer poets could master the growing corpus of the poetic tradition, these schools established more limited canons. The self-consciousness of much of this poetry led to bookishness, a defect that poems of heroic abandon sought to transcend.

Against bookishness, the poet-statesman Su Shi 蘇軾 (1037–1101) confronted the sorrow of exile with a defiant imagination. Su balanced his reverence for past tradition with a critical spirit evident in the first and third stanzas of his first of "Two Poems on Reading Meng Jiao's Poetry" 讀孟郊詩二首:

> At night I read the poems of Meng Jiao.
> Characters fine like the hairs of a cow.
> The cold lamp shines as my eyes blur and cloud.
> Exquisite lines are rare to be found.

> At first [reading Meng's poetry] is like eating small fish.
> What I get does not recompense my toil.
> Or like trying to boil numerous crabs, all told
> At the end of the day nothing but hollow claws I hold.

In the fifth and final stanza, Su suggests an alternative.

> Why should I strain my ears
> To listen to these autumn insects howl and pine?
> Better to set the poetry aside for now
> And drink my jade-colored dregs of wine.

With both Buddhist and Daoist leanings, Su's expansive attitude developed the mode of "heroic abandon," a style that would later be contrasted to the delicate and suggestive style of much poetry.

Such distinctions and related debates about the purposes of poetry intensified after printed texts brought poetry to more of the literate population, and major thirteenth-century manuals spread poetry writing. In one camp an influential movement to revive antiquity emphasized competence in "poetic style" as learned from earlier masters, especially those of the Tang. Concerned about what they saw as the mundane and imitative nature of much poetry after the Tang, and wary of imitation's suppression of creativity, a rival school championed individual expression, emotions over moral intentions, and a hedonistic approach to literature. As literary coteries debated the relative virtues of method and individual creativity, even the individualists valued received method, but they likened method to the raft in the Buddhist parable that can be left behind after crossing a river. Once poetry societies gained influence, with some welcoming even women and commoners, these debates reached a large population of readers.

As women increasingly wrote and commented on poetry, by the mid-seventeenth century, women writers such as Wang Duanshu 王端淑 and Huang Yuanjie 黃媛介 were forging unconventional lives. Supported by male mentors, companionate marriages, and literati families who financed their works' publication, these women wrote prose as well as poetry, tutored other women gentry, and edited anthologies. They also enjoyed boat trips in which they drank and exchanged verses, and collections such as Wang Duanshu's *Extracanonical Poetry by Famous Women* 名媛詩緯 (1667) broke new ground in promoting women's writing. In a preface to Wang's volume, her husband gently chides her neglect of household duties, but records testify to her faithful solicitude toward her husband and his concubines.

In contrast to earlier women poets, who wrote mostly about love and longing, some of these women wrote about loyalty to the Ming dynasty. New confidence in individual expression led to brave reworkings of traditional tropes, as can be seen in Huang Yuanjie's poem "Written to Accompany a Small Landscape Painting" 題山水小幅:

> Enough of ascending tall towers to gaze at mountains green,
> Ashamed, I've learned these years to close the gate

And with pale ink to limn a dim vague trace
Of a lonely peak felt in the space between.

The inward turn of Huang's poem suggests the difficult position
of poets facing the Manchu conquest and early Qing rule. Divided
between resistance and accommodation, literati increasingly
connected aesthetic commitments to political allegiances.
Whereas earlier schools often formed around places and master-
disciple relationships, during the high Qing period theoretical
principles took precedence. Intent on countering revived
archaism, for example, the master poet Yuan Mei 袁枚 (1716–97)
championed "native sensibility," and, as these lines suggest, a very
modern individualism:

A person is born to live with delight;
What pleases a soul depends on its type.
Yet one must act in time with the seasons,
Each in accord with his own guiding reasons.

Chapter 3
Classical narrative: history, jottings, and tales of the strange

China's earliest narratives date at least as far back as the fifth century BCE, yet it remains unclear just when Chinese writers began consciously crafting fiction. Though not considered creative writing, many of these narratives present powerful visions of feelings, ghosts, spirits, and other natural and supernatural phenomena. Yet Confucius's imperative "to transmit without creating" (*Analects* 7.2) encouraged a conception of history as merely facts to be recorded, a presumption reflected in the terse historical annals later attributed to him. Stories not based in history were derided as "little talk" 小說, a term that much later became the modern word for fiction. But whereas contemporary discussions of fiction often include parables and fictionalized episodes from the early historical and philosophical canons, few of these works would have been denigrated to the level of "little talk" as defined by early historians. For the historian Ban Gu 班固 (32–92 CE), "little talk" was merely "gossip of the alleys," records useful for political but not literary purposes, and the label was for centuries a term of mild disparagement.

Yet fictional elements can be seen in China's earliest sustained narrative, *Zuo's Commentary* 左傳, a work attributed to the blind historian Zuo Qiuming 左丘明 (ca. fourth century BCE). In the first of its year-by-year entries, a long passage celebrates the possibility of redemption through filial love. Hated by his mother, the Duke of Zhuang overturns a plot in which she conspires to overthrow him, then confines her and vows not to see her until they reach the Yellow Springs, the land of the dead. Deeply moved by a border guard's sharing of food with his own mother, Zhuang laments, "You have a mother to take things to. Alas, I alone have none!" When Zhuang confesses his regret over his vow, the guard encourages him to dig a tunnel down to the springs in order to meet his mother while honoring his vow. As his mother emerges from the tunnel, mother and son exchange verses of joy, and the passage ends with a comment on the guard's supreme filial piety.

Because formal distinctions between history and fiction were made only in the eighth century, when Liu Zhiji 劉知幾 (661–721) distinguished respectable historical writing from "witty yet petty talk" in his *Generalities on History* 史通 (710), many scholars divide early Chinese narrative into two branches according to content rather than truth-value. History presents public issues: military, political, diplomatic, and court-related affairs; while fiction details private lives. Yet many early texts defy this division. Though concerned with an imperial inspection, for example, the historical romance-travelogue *Biography of Mu, Son of Heaven* 穆天子傳 (ca. fourth century BCE) is full of fictional motifs, as is the supernatural geographical work *Classics of the Mountains and Seas* 山海經 (ca. 320 BCE).

How did literati understand the role and purpose of such texts during the thirteen centuries before the conscious crafting of fiction? And what do we make of a tale such as this one selected by the court historian Gan Bao 干寶 (fl. 320) for his collection *In Search of Spirits* 搜神記?

> One night Su Yi, a woman of Luling good at midwifery, was suddenly abducted by a tiger. After going six or seven *li*, they arrived at a large field where the tiger put her down on the earth and knelt to keep watch. Su Yi saw a tigress in labor but powerless to deliver. Crawling about as if she wanted to die, she looked up in Yi's

direction. Yi found it strange, but she explored and pulled out three cubs. The births complete, a tigress carried Yi home on her back. Thereafter wild game was many times delivered inside her gate.

This brief tale is representative of what would later be called "records of the strange" 志怪. By borrowing the documentary style of official history, recorder-compilers such as Gan Bao sought to benefit from history's prestige in order to present unusual phenomena. In dignifying the tigers with compassion, resourcefulness, and gratitude, the tale situates the animals as moral exemplars. Such tales, transmitted orally by storytellers, then penned by literati, shared a common purpose with official history. Such records bolstered belief in a benevolent universe in which, thanks to traditional morality and proper ritual behavior, human actions could be meaningful and ethical behavior rewarded.

Ritual: histories of praise and blame

In ancient China, writing's primary function appears to have been to aid memory. During the Zhou dynasty (1027–256 BCE), scribes in the Ministry of Rites recorded ancestral rituals, dynastic decrees, official exchanges, and the words and deeds of the ruler, the "Son of Heaven." By the mid–Warring States period (475–221 BCE), writing also took on a moralistic function. In the face of war and the reorganization of states, thinkers increasingly appealed to historical precedents to promote the ideal of a patterned and ordered universe. Eager to account for change in terms of moral and natural causes, rulers granted authority and prestige to historians' projects whose accountings would legitimate their governments.

To reinforce the traditionalist Confucian belief in morality's connection to heaven's will, early historians selectively recorded events to convey praise for their patrons and blame on their rivals. If, for example, a battle occurred before or after an astrological constellation indicating their kingdom's ascendency, the date was falsified. While the dating of events served from the beginning to support political ends, such ideological uses of writing expanded as philosophical texts such as the *Zhuangzi* and the *Mencius* demonstrated that the stirring nature of narrative made it a powerful tool of instruction.

More than impart information, the works of early historians presumed to draw moral lessons from the past. Particularly influential were histories configured as commentaries on the *Springs and Autumns*, one of the "Five Classics" attributed to Confucius. Taking the annals' terse entries to convey moral judgments through omissions, double entendre, and subtleties of style, these commentaries established a normative ethical system based on the practice of appropriate ritual. In these histories, causality follows the principle of recompense: moral and ritual transgressions cause war and strife, whereas honoring ritual and history leads toward peace and justice.

Learning from history depends on taking seriously the force of words, and *Zuo's Commentary*, China's first history to combine records of events with dialogues, bears witness to the power of language. Faced with a proposal to destroy a district school where people criticize his administration, for example, the ruler Zichan reasons that it is better to learn from than try to silence one's subjects:

> I have heard of reducing grievances by means of loyalty and kindness; I have not heard of preventing grievances by exercising power. Why not stop such criticism right away, you might ask. But doing so would be like trying to prevent a river from overflowing with a dike. Should a big burst occur, those harmed would be many, and I would not be able to save them. Just as it would be better to make a small opening to let the water flow out, so I listen to criticism as a remedy.

The passage ends with a comment attributed to Confucius upon hearing the account: "Judging by the situation, when people say that Zichan is not benevolent, I will not believe it." Amid what is mostly straightforward historical narration, such occasional judgments (eighty-four in all) present a distinct point of view and indicate the recorder-narrator's moral purposes, i.e., to promote the belief that the evil meet with disaster and the good with reward.

Many early histories give pride of place to the powerful role of historian-persuaders in safeguarding such moral justice. In the *Discourses of the States* 國語 (fourth century BCE), for example, rulers may ignore counsel informed by wisdom of natural and historical processes, but only at their own and their loved ones' peril. When a duke ignores a historian's prediction that a military victory will bring misfortune and takes the defeated chief's daughter to be his consort, he unleashes her plot to depose the Crown Prince Shensheng and establish her own son as heir. Shensheng stands above all for reverence for parents, the virtue seen as the basis for all others, but his virtue is also his undoing. For him, the imperatives of filial piety trump even survival, and though he learns of the consort's machinations, he refuses to take any measures that might dishonor his father. Since he ultimately hangs himself in the ancestral temple, what is a reader to make of the eloquent speeches by three ministers who debate the consort's plan? After one recalls the historian's prediction, and a second advises following orders without questioning, a third objects: "He who serves his ruler follows what is right but does not flatter the ruler's delusions. If the ruler is deluded the people will be misled, and if the people are misled they will abandon virtue." Though the individual Shensheng dies a tragic devotee of filial piety, the narrative may imply that historical reflection itself, and the role of brave ministers, can check moral decadence and help the pendulum swing back toward virtue.

Earlier texts often present moral judgments, possibly added by later editors, but these judgments are generally attributed to Confucius (or to a "gentleman" taken to be Confucius) and thus do not foreground authorship. The first work to document a more conscious conception of authorship is the masterpiece of early history, the *Historical Records* 史記 (ca. 100 BCE), completed by the historian Sima Qian 司馬遷 (145–87? BCE). Entrusted by his dying father Sima Tan not only to continue their ancestors' work as court chroniclers but to expand the historian's role to embrace history's great men and their deeds, Sima Qian's dedication was put to the test when he was accused of libel against the emperor for defending a defeated general. Condemned to castration, rather than take the customary recourse of suicide, he endured the maiming in order to further his father's mission.

Sima's history—albeit a compilation of earlier historical sources—is pathbreaking for supplementing year-by-year annals with biographies that allow for the characterization of individuals and groups. Over half a million characters long (fifteen times the length of this book), the work's 130 chapters cover 2,500 years of history in small, overlapping units. As the first and most inventive of the twenty-five dynastic histories, the *Historical Records* established many conventions and themes followed by later historians. Combining lively narrative and quoted discourse, the fast-moving language brings the biographies to life. In addition to individual biographies of rulers, ministers, assassins, and others, Sima offers collective biographies of cruel and upright officials, scholars, wandering knights, toadies, jesters, and avaricious merchants, as well as his own "autobiographical postface of the Lord Grand Historian."

In seeking to educate his country, Sima expressed subtle criticisms by dramatizing accounts he esteemed and omitting or tersely recording those he condemned. The formula "The Lord Grand Historian says," usually at the end of chapters, introduces comments on the accounts. "How sorrowful!" or "Alas, how pitiful," the historian exclaims, guiding his readers' response. These emotional reactions make Sima's history China's first to introduce the historian himself as a character and commentator.

(Many of the later dynastic histories set forth events more impersonally, employing a kind of narrator by committee.)

Sima testified to his authorial ambitions in his "Letter Replying to Ren An" 報仁安書, a remarkable first-person account of his personal history, views, and frustrations: "It was my desire, by an investigation of the workings of affairs divine and human, and a thorough knowledge of the historical process of change, to create a philosophy of my own." With these lines, Sima Qian poses both history and historiography as matters of human decision.

The tradition of belles lettres

Whereas most writing during the Han dynasty served practical purposes, the collapse of centralized government in 220 CE occasioned an explosion of permissible subjects and forms. From the third to the sixth centuries writing rose in stature as literati built a tradition of belles lettres. Because respect for the classics discouraged large-scale philosophizing, this tradition was made up largely of envois, essays, letters, travel writing, and other short prose pieces. This tradition was codified in anthologies and theoretical treatises that developed specific genres, literary lineages, and evaluative terms.

In what may be the earliest conscious discourse on literature, the first emperor of the Wei Kingdom (220–65), Cao Pi 曹丕 (187–226), celebrated literature as the greatest accomplishment in managing a country. Contrasting the endurance of literary works with the inevitable exhaustion of a lifespan and the passing of honor and pleasure with the body's death, Cao cast writing as a way of addressing the terror of time's passing. Cao particularly praised strong character and clear vital energy (*qi*). He took *qi* to be inborn, and literary criticism would henceforth be profoundly marked by practices of "appraising character" based on concepts of talent, physical appearances, dispositions, and styles.

7. As the literati coalesced as a class, many demonstrated deep bonds of friendship and mutual support, as in Qiu Ying's 仇英 painting (ca. 1550) depicting a poor scholar receiving a gift of a donkey bought after scholar-friends pooled money.

At least since Cao Pi's discourse, literati began to reflect on the function of literature and, through these reflections, to construct themselves as a class. This self-consciousness led the twentieth-century writer Lu Xun 魯迅 (1881–1936) to identify the early third century as "literature's age of self-awareness." While the importance of government service lent particular esteem to official writings such as memorials of thanks, disapproval, or congratulations, this period also saw a rise in the therapeutic function of literature, as writers addressed personal anxieties and sentiments. In "Memorial Expressing My Situation" 陳情表, for example, the scholar Li Mi 李密 (224–87) offers an emotional first-person narrative to request leave from official duties. Humbly submitting that "it is with filial piety that the Sage Dynasty governs all under heaven," Li explains, "Your subject is forty-four this year; [my] Grandmother Liu ninety-six. Hence the days are many for me to complete my season of service to your Majesty, but few indeed to repay her."

By the fourth century, writers recorded simple short "jottings" 筆記 they did not present as history or philosophy. United by their use of the classical language, these jottings were favored by scholar-gentlemen not only for historical anecdotes, social commentary, musings, travel notes, and contemplations of nature, but also for diaries, jokes and what we would now call fiction. Many of these works were formed by gradual accretion, one of several factors that worked against a concept of consciously created fiction. Yet in privileging narrative over discursive materials, these works branched off from history in their focus on imaginative reality.

Records of the strange

The new inventiveness of "records of the strange" may have stemmed from desires to harness the potency of strange phenomena to promote moral norms. To bolster belief in their jottings, collector-recorders often followed historical chronologies and used the names of actual places and people. Yet it would be hard not to admire their works' imaginative crafting. Many of these tales describe strange occurrences associated with natural gods, ghosts, spirits, Buddhist monks and nuns, Daoist adepts, and fantastical people, places, and events. As Gan Bao put it in the preface to his fourth-century *In Search of Spirits*, he hoped the records he had collected would demonstrate that "the Way of spirits is not false," and offer sources wherein future scholars could "let their hearts wander and their eyes dwell."

Though later sometimes considered "the birth of fiction," records of the strange were in their time a form of unofficial or "leftover" history. These records borrowed many formal features from historical works, including the use of prophetic dreams, omens, and prognostications, yet their narrative style permitted more complex plots and more psychological presentations of character. Some of the 464 records in Gan's collection, like the story of Su Yi and the tigers, are minimal sketches in a few dozen words, but others are sophisticated tales depicting numerous conflicts and character types. Moreover, whereas stories such as Su Yi's depict people and beasts in a single moral universe, other records posit boundaries between them. Perhaps to control the animal instincts of humans, many accounts used animals to inspire human morality.

Like Su Yi's tale, many stories of the strange revolve around values of reciprocity, recompense, and revenge, all translations of the central concept of *bao* 報. The tale of Dong Zhaozhi, also from Gan's collection, rewards its eponymous protagonist for saving an ant's life. In a dream, a black-clad leader followed by a hundred men appears, offers his thanks and urges, "If ever in anxious difficulty, you should call on me to appear." Ten years later, after Zhaozhi is unjustly jailed, he remembers the Ant King's words, and so takes a few ants in hand and appeals to them. In a second dream, the leader in black instructs him to flee to the hills and await an amnesty. Upon waking, Zhaozhi finds that ants have eaten away his shackles, and he flees to the hills, soon to be pardoned.

Although some tales present straightforward morals, the absence of a predetermined value system makes other stories more challenging. Certain motifs and structures suggest a tragic tension between heaven's will and even the noblest of mortal desires. Celebrated as a tale of extraordinary love and devotion, "Han Ping and His Wife" 韓憑夫婦 (also from *In Search of Spirits*) is also a lamentation on the helplessness of commoners against the powerful. While the story suggests the power of writing to confront injustice, it also highlights ambiguities of interpretation. After the king abducts Ping's wife, her enigmatic letter to Ping reveals the unpredictable trajectory of writing's moral power.

> Excessive rain, continuous rain.
> Broad is the river, its waters deep.
> The sun appears like my heart's aim.

When the puzzled king shows his counselors the intercepted letter, a minister interprets the excessive rain as her ongoing worry and

longing for her husband, the broad river as their powerlessness to
see each other, and her heart's aim as a resolution to die. Though
the tale leaves unclear whether Ping has received his wife's letters,
he commits suicide. His wife then lets her clothes rot, so they rip
when attendants try to catch her after she throws herself from a
tower to her death. Angered by a letter requesting that her bones
be buried in her husband's grave, the king orders facing graves.
Overnight large catalpa trees grow atop the two grave mounds, and
in ten days their trunks bend toward each other, their branches
embrace, and their roots intertwine. Two mandarin ducks settle in
the trees, press close their necks, and cry woefully. Moved by their
cries, the local people grieve for the couple, call the catalpa "the
tree of mutual longing," and come to view the birds as the couple's
reincarnated souls.

The tale also underscores what it means to have intentions and
carry them out. The woman's patience in letting her clothes rot
shows her decisiveness, and her letter informing the king that
she benefits by dying proclaims her control over her destiny.
Choosing to resist the king in the only way she can, she may
inspire a measure of compassion, seen in his decision to allow
nearby graves. Yet part of the tale's mystery lies in the minister's
interpretation of her first ambiguous letter. Since the word the
minister interprets as "continuous" also means "licentious," the
first line could refer to her sexual exploitation in the hands of
the king. Or, since rain and sun nurture trees, these lines might
foreshadow the embracing catalpa trees, an omen that lends
structural unity to the tale.

Recording people and crafting fiction

As records of anomalies told of alleged occurrences, jottings
appraising character generally presented sketches of supposedly
historical persons. The moral implications were often more
straightforward, as can be seen in the hundreds of records of
virtues and vices in *New Accounts of Tales of the World* 世說新語.

Compiled around 430, this anthology of erudite, humorous anecdotes and conversations includes some jottings as simple as the tale of a ruler whose chagrin over his ignorance about rice paddies leads him to cloister himself for three days. "How could one rely on its end product and not recognize its source?" Other episodes compare two men to illustrate moral qualities, character flaws, intellectual abilities, and personality types.

Tales of the World thus became an important source of "pure conversation," dialogues in which literati sought to detach from mundane politics and thus establish themselves as arbiters of refined taste. The work inspired centuries of imitations in "tales-of-the-world-style" compilations, and modern scholars see this subgenre of jottings, later called "recording people" 志人, as integral to the pursuit of elite distinction.

As more literati rejected dominant values of political service and embraced aesthetic values and pleasures, they turned to writing as a private act serving literary ends, and their prose laments, eulogies, epitaphs, and biographies joined poetry as common forms of personal expression. In "The Biography of Mr. Five Willows" 五柳先生傳, for example, the poet Tao Qian 陶潛 (365–427) parodies official biographies to present a wry autobiography mixing Daoist and Confucian values: "Placid, serene, and of few words, he envies neither glory nor gain. He is fond of reading books but does not seek to understand everything. Each time he understands a subtlety, his joy is so great that he forgets to eat." Though his dwelling is humble, his robe coarse, and "his basket and gourd often empty," Mr. Five Willows delights in writing literature and expressing his ideals.

If the conscious crafting of fiction depended in part on a conception of authorship that took shape only as the literati coalesced as a class, it seems fitting that a poet with such a clear sense of his literary identity would also compose one of the earliest examples of intentional fiction. Originally a preface to a poem, Tao's allegorical "Record of the Peach Blossom Spring"

桃花源記 tells a fable about a fisherman who follows a stream, ventures through a small opening, and discovers a utopian community secluded from his world's political strife. Admiring their contentment and generosity, the fisherman disregards their appeal for secrecy and marks his return route to report to his prefect. Yet he can never find the way again, and the fable has become a metaphor for a lost paradise.

The recognition of literature as a distinct genre and of the literati as a class owes much to the compilation of the sixth-century anthology *Selections of Literature* 文選. In his preface, the compiler Xiao Tong 蕭統 (501–31) distinguishes literature from history (which treats facts) and philosophy (which treats ideas) by literature's treatment of experience in aesthetically crafted form and language. Establishing the basic canon of poetry and short prose, this anthology became the definitive reader for most educated people. This shared corpus made it unnecessary to spell out allusions, a task left to later commentators and, together with the institution in 605 of the civil-service entrance exams, helped the literati cohere as a class.

Though *Selections of Literature* excluded "little talk," by the early Song dynasty the genre had developed to the point that the emperor commissioned a compendium of roughly seven thousand such works from the turn of the millennium to the present. Printing blocks were carved to prepare the *Extensive Records of the Era of Grand Peace* 太平廣記 (977–78). Yet moral objections halted publication, and the text was published only in 1566. (This delay may testify to fears of fiction's power.) The sole source for many stories from before the early Song, this work's belated publication greatly promoted the study of earlier fiction.

Tales of the marvelous

Despite fictional elements in the earlier records of the strange, scholars have generally followed Hu Yinglin 胡應麟 (1551–1602) in seeing the longer "tales of the marvelous" 傳奇 (literally "transmitting wonders") as China's first deliberately created fiction. Penned from the Tang dynasty (618–907) on, these tales also depict natural wonders but focus more on private life, and often explicitly identify the author and his motives for recording the tale. It's unclear whether this attention to writing represented a conscious embrace of a creative role. For while most of the core tales employ omniscient, impersonal narration, many are framed as told to the narrator by a witness, as if the story were an objective chronicle.

Building a bridge from the stories to the world of the reader, these narrative frames frequently reflect on the core story's ethical import. This emphasis on moral suasion may reveal anxieties about the status of literati identity and traditionalist Confucian values, especially as Buddhist and other ideas gained sway during the cosmopolitan Tang dynasty. In this way, these tales, written in the classical language, share an affinity with the movement to reject ornate parallel prose and return to the "ancient-style" prose of the pre-Han and Han classics.

Given the presentation of conflicting values and voices in these tales, however, the final moral may have been designed to render a tale more respectable and thus increase its chances of dissemination. The core stories nonetheless often focus on the characters' psychology in ways that surpass the more conventional moral frame. Dissenting voices also emerge within the direct dialogue or in poems and letters written by the characters, often the richest sources of characterization.

Written by and for literati, these classical-language tales often explicitly privilege the pursuit of learning and success in civil service examinations. Yet they also evince growing concern for personal feelings that challenge normative values and class distinctions. One of the most memorable critiques of conventional paths to success is Shen Jiji's 沈既濟 (ca. 740–ca. 800) "The World Inside a Pillow" 枕中記 (781), a rewriting of a brief sketch from *In Search of Spirits*. Shen's story, written at a time when expansion of the education system produced far more scholars than the bureaucracy could employ, opens with an encounter at an inn between an old Daoist monk and a young scholar named Lu. Though they talk happily, Lu sighs over his tattered clothes and laments having been born at the wrong time. When the monk points out that he is neither suffering nor ill, he bemoans his failure to achieve renown, glory, or prosperity.

After the monk offers him a pillow he assures will bring the honor and happiness of his aspirations, Lu awakens to find his fortunes changed. He marries a maiden from a noble family and holds a series of ever higher official positions, at one point winning his compatriots' praise by building a canal. Twice he suffers slander and banishment, part of the trajectory of a great official, and reacts by becoming a recluse. Once his name is cleared, he rises to even higher positions, watches his five sons achieve success and, falling ill at the end of his lavish life, writes a letter of resignation that conveys the story's satire on traditional values. But then Lu awakens to find himself back with the Daoist monk, the innkeeper's millet still not fully cooked. Lu asks if his full life has been but a dream. "Such are the affairs of the human world," the monk replies, and though initially disappointed, Lu thanks him: "Now I completely know the reckonings of grace and disgrace, the pattern of gains and loss, and the passions of life and death. Thus, mentor, you have restrained my desires and I dare not receive this teaching."

As in Shen's story, the most fully rounded characters in these tales are often men who cultivate scholarly pursuits. They write clear prose, paint, do calligraphy, and pass the civil-service exams. When women characters are developed, they are often educated courtesans or "fox spirits." While such women may support scholars preparing for exams, they are often depicted as dangerous temptresses. Many tales portray women transforming into fox spirits or specters, a motif that may betray fears of the ties of love,

"The Story of Yingying"

"The Story of Yingying" 鶯鶯傳 (804) may be the best-known Chinese love story. It is also a foremost example of the major subgenre of "scholar-beauty tales" depicting the rise and fall of a love affair between an aspiring young scholar and a beautiful courtesan. Attributed to the poet Yuan Zhen 元稹 (779–831), the tale dramatizes the conflict between Confucian duty and the growing cult of feeling. After the protagonist Zhang uses his connections to protect his fellow lodgers at a monastery, he becomes infatuated with the radiant Yingying. Though Zhang's impatience to seduce Yingying leads her first to tease and then refuse him, she returns to abandon herself to him. As her initial reserve and severity give way to passionate desire, and after Zhang sends a poem on "encountering an immortal," they enjoy regular trysts in the western wing until Zhang departs for the capital to take his examinations. Though silent in lovemaking, Yingying writes an eloquent love letter, her attempt to control the affair. But the tale ends sadly, as Zhang abandons Yingying on the grounds that his virtue is "not sufficient" to withstand his lover's bewitching evil. In so doing, he casts suspicion on all beautiful women: "If those destined by heaven to be exquisite beings do not destroy themselves, then they will inevitably bring harm upon others." Although the tale is hardly unique in demonizing beautiful women, and though Zhang's friends, including the narrator, may support his privileging of duty, the tale's inclusion of Yingying's moving poem-letter also promotes the value of love. Compared to her depth of feeling, Zhang's rationalizations seem wooden. Among numerous later adaptations of the story are a thirteenth-century version, five times longer, which makes Yingying's maid a major character, and a beloved drama, *Story of the Western Wing*.

or of passion more generally, as well as beliefs that men need to preserve their vital force through sexual restraint.

Despite exemplary devotion and other virtues, such women characters almost always meet with sad ends, as if undeserving of human concern because of their supernatural powers. In Shen's "The Tale of Miss Ren" 任氏傳 (781), for example, a loyal fox spirit honors her pledge of loyalty to Cheng Liu, a poor man who loves her, despite her growing affection for his more sophisticated friend Yin. Moreover, although a shamaness warns her against traveling westward, she obediently accompanies Cheng until, when dogs attack her, she assumes her original fox form only to be devoured by the pack. The story ends with the narrator naming himself as the author (explaining that he has heard the story from Yin) and marveling at Ren's virtue and faithfulness unto death. He decries that Cheng, not a man of sensitivity, enjoyed only her beauty and failed to grasp her emotional character. "Had he been a scholar of deep learning, rather than stopping at appreciating her outward bearing, he could have rubbed shoulders with the principles of natural transformations, investigated the boundary between spirits and humans, and transmitted her wondrous feelings in beautiful prose writings." Such moral commentaries often end these tales, but seldom restore the moral order disrupted within the core story.

Although tales of revenge are common in early histories, these tales of the marvelous also include China's first detective-type crime stories. In Li Gongze's 李公佐 (770–850) "The Tale of Xie Xiao'e" 謝小娥傳, for example, a woman disguises herself as a man to avenge the murders of her father and husband. Unraveling conundrums the departed communicate to Xiao'e in her dreams, the story's narrator deciphers the roots of the Chinese characters in the two murderers' names. Xiao'e then hires herself as a manservant to the bandits and, after two years of collecting evidence, beheads one and helps the authorities execute the other. Although such vigilante justice might raise concerns about killing suspects based on a dream, the tale ends with "a gentleman" commenting on her virtue and the author-narrator's account of his decision to write the story.

Questions of justice and loyalty also arise in Pei Xing's 裴鉶 late ninth-century tale "The Tale of Nie Yinniang" 聶隱娘傳, one of the earliest tales of swordspeople. Abducted by a mendicant nun for five years of apprenticeship, the maiden Yinniang becomes a skilled assassin equipped with a dagger embedded in her skull. Yet when sent to kill a viceroy who turns out to possess great wisdom, she switches allegiance, and he courteously accepts her apology. "Don't feel guilty," he offers, "You were conscientiously serving your master." Knights-errant who rescue the downtrodden and redress injustice populate a mid-sixteenth century anthology, *Tales of Chivalrous Swordspeople* 劍俠傳. Yet unlike the cross-dressing Xie Xiao'e or the masculinized swordswoman Yinniang, the heroines of these tales often remain feminine.

Later classical tales

Most poetry, essays, and prose continued to be composed in classical Chinese into the early twentieth century. As classical language fiction came to share the stage with vernacular fiction (from the twelfth century on), works written in the demanding highbrow language became more marked. By writing in the literary language, authors proclaimed their alignment with traditional Confucian values such as moderation, filial piety, and righteousness. These classical tales were often presented as reliable accounts heard from relatives and literati friends, monks, and commoners. Scholars also increasingly collected such stories to support specific philosophies. The historian Hong Mai 洪邁 (1123–1202), for example, devoted sixty years to compiling the then-largest collection of oral anecdotes, *Records of the Listener* 夷堅志, organized according to a neo-Confucian belief in a patterned universe.

Defying such neat organization and blurring the distinction between records of the strange and tales of the marvelous, Pu Songling's 蒲松齡 (1640–1715) *Strange Stories from a Leisure Studio* 聊齋志異 (1766) is the pinnacle of classical-language tales. Despite Pu's erudition, demonstrated in early success at the district-level civil service exams, he never passed the provincial level, let alone the capital level necessary to be granted an official position. This professional disappointment, as well as concerns about injustice, may have fueled Pu's scathing satires on the pretenses of power.

In nearly five hundred tales and anecdotes about lovers, ghosts, fox spirits, and demons, Pu's satirical humor, broad range of themes, and soft eroticism dramatize life's uncanny nature. As characters cross boundaries between the natural and supernatural, the stories also bring out the fluidity of selfhood and sexuality.

The tales may surprise in their matter-of-fact presentation of sex, the mobility of erotic attachments, and the guiltless taking of multiple lovers. Whereas certain female characters, often ghosts and fox spirits, cannot help but drain and sicken their lovers, the most humane of these spirits show remarkable self-awareness and integrity. "Lotus Fragrance" 蓮香 tells of a scholar who almost dies of sexual excess as he juggles two libidinous lovers, one of whom turns out to be a fox spirit, the other a ghost. Joining forces to save his life, the two rivals happily share him until the ghost inexplicably disappears. When she is reborn into a wealthy family as an eligible young woman, the scholar seeks her hand in marriage. And to assuage his fox lover's jealousy, he marries her too. The three enjoy a ménage-à-trois until the fox spirit dies in childbirth, leaving the reincarnated ghost to raise her son. Then, after some years, an old woman brings the couple a maiden who turns out to be the reincarnated fox. Reunited in close friendship over two lifetimes, they consummate their solidarity by reinterring the ghost's original bones to commingle with the fox's in a single grave.

"If ghosts and foxes are like this," asks a commentator, "what harm can they possibly do?" Such commentaries generally intersperse Chinese pre-modern fiction to underscore Confucian values. When the fox spirit explains that hearty young men can restore their *qi* three days after lovemaking but that daily indulgence will cause harm, another commentary cautions: "Wise counsel. Young people, take heed of this!" Such passages and comments reveal prevalent anxieties about sexuality and especially about men's vulnerability to women. Yet Pu's stories also radically depart from the tradition in allowing happy endings to supernatural women characters.

In Pu's masterpiece "Jiaona" 嬌娜, the members of a fox-spirit family combine their supernatural powers with the best of human sentiment, displaying erudition, medical skills, and moral rectitude. The tale, translated by John Minford as "Grace and Pine," begins when Kong Xueli, a mandarin scholar stranded penniless far from home, agrees to tutor a mysterious wealthy young gentleman, Huangfu. Kong awakens to sexual desire when he takes a fancy to Huangfu's maid, then becomes utterly smitten by Huangfu's beautiful sister, Grace (Jiaona). When a painful inflammation almost kills Kong, Grace cures him through surgery and sorcery. Yet after this symbolic deflowering rife with sexual tension, Grace disappears and Kong's lovesick yearning reduces him to listlessness. Because Grace is underage, Huangfu arranges a marriage to his equally stunning cousin Pine, a substitution that redirects but cannot contain Kong's erotic tension. And as Huangfu transports the newlyweds to Kong's family home by soaring on the wind, Kong finally realizes that his friend is no mortal human.

Kong's good fortune increases over the years as he passes the highest civil-service exam, wins an appointment as a judge, and has a son with Pine. But he never forgets how Grace earlier saved his life, and his gratitude is put to the test when Huangfu explains that his family faces disaster. "We are all foxes," Huangfu at last reveals, "and today a terrible thunderstorm is about to strike us. If you are willing to risk your own life to protect us, we may yet be saved. If not, then take your child now and go; do not let yourself be caught up in our fate." Kong vows to live or die with his in-laws and, wielding a sword, proves his manhood by sacrificing his life to stop a hideous monster from abducting Grace. After the foxes magically revivify him, they all agree to return home with him except Grace, prevented by her duties to her husband's parents. A deus ex machina fulfills their wishes when a natural calamity claims her in-laws, allowing Grace to join the others. "Huangfu and Grace were installed in a separate compound in the garden, where they kept their gate permanently shut, only opening it for Kong and Pine."

For all their eerie mystery, these tales often end with such idylls and the inherent suggestion that the principles of a benevolent universe still prevail. Such fantastical tales may cast doubt on conventional paths to success, but they continue to reinforce Confucian values. Recalling Sima Qian's *Historical Records*, chapter-end comments by "the Historian of the Strange" offer trenchant social criticisms, especially concerning the dangers of pretension. And characters such as Kong might even serve as alter egos for Pu Songling and for readers who would identify with erudite, ethical figures. As his devotion to his vulpine in-laws clearly trumps concerns about official status, like the scholar in "The World Inside a Pillow," Kong learns through professional reversals not to overly esteem worldly rewards. Moreover, his ardent yet platonic relationship with Grace (which some commentators see as the main love story) opens him to an intimacy and wonder beyond physical sex. As Pu's refined language keeps the author-narrator at an impersonal remove, his tales' masterful control projects a subtle sensuality redolent of dreams and private fantasy.

Chapter 4

Vernacular drama and fiction: gardens, bandits, and dreams

Bandits in the garden

In *Dream of the Red Chamber* 紅樓夢 (1792), China's most celebrated novel, the protagonist and his female companions dwell in his family's protected Grand Contemplation Garden. Symbols of wealth's pleasures, sensual indulgence, and longings for immortality, Chinese gardens traditionally represent sequestered miniatures of an ordered universe. Though corruption rages in the rest of the family compound and in the mundane "world of red dust" beyond, it is primarily in the garden that the novel explores profound tensions between karmic destiny, worldly duty, and emotional attachments.

The discovery of a purse embroidered with a pornographic image exposes the garden's infiltration by wanton forces, and the family's subsequent panic betrays rampant anxieties about the vulnerability of moral order. Testifying to heightened fears of the temptations of greed and lust, works such as *Dream of the Red Chamber* unsettle the classical tradition's deep philosophical optimism. Much classical literature, steeped in a Confucian faith in a benevolent world, presumed the viability of a harmonious moral Way. But literary sources as early as the eleventh century suggest that only a far more conflicted faith survived the fall of the glorious Tang dynasty (618–906) and the material and social transformations of the Song (960–1279).

8. A refuge from the "world of red dust," the Chinese garden offers a microcosm of a patterned universe. The rocks in this garden could symbolize mountains, and the pond a sea.

By the Song, the growth of cities and a money economy drove the proliferation of specialized occupations. Thanks to the eighth-century invention of book printing, literacy and education increased among a burgeoning middle class of urban merchants, artisans, and other professionals. And though records are limited because of performers' low social status, a vibrant entertainment sector supported guilds of professional storytellers, cultivated courtesans, and theater troupes. These technological and social changes fostered the rise of a written vernacular whose more everyday language made literature accessible beyond the literati class. Most serious writings continued to use the elite literary language (and would until the twentieth century), but from the thirteenth century, vernacular language became prevalent in popular fiction, drama, and songs.

These works voice a growing skepticism about reconciling ethical conduct with human passions. Though literati still penned most of this literature, many works now reflected the values of an expanded and less cohesive audience. As more literati vied for limited civil service positions, many disappointed candidates found themselves underemployed and marginalized from politics. During the Ming dynasty (1368–1644), the literati's status as a distinct class became more pronounced as accelerating economic growth led to a further separation of governmental, economic, and cultural spheres characteristic of early modern societies. Formerly the state had been the main patron and publisher; from about the sixteenth century commercial printers actively published mass-produced popular literature.

Although vernacular works still convey ethical lessons, their pointed depictions of folly and ignorance often question the power of moral cultivation to contain the dangers of excessive passions. Departing from the emotional restraint of many earlier poems and narratives, dramas with dozens of scenes and novels with sometimes more than one hundred chapters place characters' passions and actions within large, complex frameworks. As such works increasingly portray conflicts between dominant values, they evince a new pluralism in their explorations of love, acquisitiveness, and pursuits of honor and happiness.

Oral performance literatures: show and tell

Dramas and novels evolved from a long storytelling tradition rooted in ancient court entertainers, shadow plays, comic dialogues, and various forms of farce. Because written records overrepresent literati and their values, less is known about the oral transmission of such genres. Yet literate readers were still a minority; popular stories, folklore, and jokes spread largely through oral performances. Performing alone or at times in duos or trios, storytellers were less costly than theater troupes, and the inexpensive entertainment they provided reached large popular audiences.

As Buddhism gained influence during the Tang dynasty, translations of Buddhist texts from India brought new forms and influenced the rise of written vernacular Chinese. Often performed together with pictures and music, "transformational texts" 變文 mixed prose and verse to retell parables such as the story of Mulian (Mahāmaudgalyāyana in Sanskrit), a disciple who releases his mother from agony in hell.

Scholars call the many genres that evolved from such texts "prosimetric," literally "tell-and-sing literature" 說唱文學. "Verses for plucking (lutes)," often written and performed by women, frequently portrayed court intrigues, including cross-dressing women who ace the civil service exams to win official appointments. Among other prosimetric genres are Buddhist legends performed by nuns ("treasured scrolls"), and new spoken-language arias used for poetry, "medleys," and dramas.

Developed in Song-era entertainment districts, medleys employ short spoken prose to explain longer sung passages. Periodic cliffhangers may have marked pauses for the storyteller to collect money or to entice the audience back for a multiday performance. The refinement of this popular genre can be seen in the *Western Wing Medley*. This eight-chapter rewriting of the ninth-century "Story of Yingying" (see chap. 3) expands the plot and ends with the lovers eloping, reversing the earlier tale's lauding of duty over feeling.

Though not well known itself, this medley inspired the most famous northern drama, Wang Shifu's 王實甫 late thirteenth-century *Story of the Western Wing* 西廂記. Widely loved for honoring private emotional relations over conventional duty, Wang's opera conveys unprecedented sympathy for erotic love. Despite its twenty-one acts, the drama feels unified through the image of the moon (evoked more than fifty times), its theme of recurring cycles, and its focus on the lovers' pathos. As the lovers' arias eulogize their emotional journey from infatuation through hope and disappointment to ultimate rapture, the drama also suggests adversity's power to deepen attachment.

Variety musicals

By the Yuan dynasty (1279–1368), dramatizations of human folly and vice regularly combined verse, classical prose, and colloquial dialogue with music, mime, and dance. Indeed, until the early twentieth century, when "spoken drama" developed partly through Western influence, Chinese drama was usually opera. Many operas were derived from tales of the marvelous, and themes included court intrigues, crime and retribution, "scholar-beauty tales," and Daoist or Buddhist salvation.

Traditional drama aimed not for realism but to convey emotions through symbolic conventions. Bringing out the artificial and even illusory nature of human experience, these operas were self-consciously melodramatic. Using standardized symbols and formulas, they featured stock characters (sometimes played by either gender): the male and female leads, trusted servants, and various older men, including naive pedants, bumbling physicians, swindlers, and corrupt officials. Upon their first appearance, characters often introduced themselves, related the play's backstory, or recapped the action thus far, but the drama generally centered more on emotion than action.

Governed by these conventions, opera flourished under the Yuan. Drama troupes performed in theaters, in private homes, and at secular and temple festivals. In northern "variety plays" 雜劇 (literally "mixed drama"), the lead sings four suites of arias, while spoken monologues, dialogues, and action move the plot along. After the customary climax in the third act, the closing act usually restores social harmony, yet these resolutions seldom dispel the drama's moral queries.

Skepticism about the world of officialdom pervades dramas such as Ma Zhiyuan's 馬致遠 (ca. 1250–1323) *Yellow Millet Dream* 黃粱夢,

a reworking of the eighth-century tale "The World Inside a Pillow" (see chap. 3). Even more scathing is Ma's portrayal of a court painter's venality in *Autumn in the Han Palace* 漢宮秋. Based on a historical account often reprised in poems and paintings, Ma's opera retells the legend of Wang Zhaojun, a palace beauty loved by the Emperor Yuan (r. 48–33 BCE) but sacrificed to the *Realpolitik* of "appeasing the barbarians by marriage."

The drama opens on the unscrupulous Mao Yanshou, commissioned to identify beauties, disfiguring Zhaojun's portrait when her peasant family refuses to bribe him. Seeing only the portrait, the emperor disregards her for a decade until he discovers the neglected beauty playing her lute, perceives her depths, and falls in love. His perfidy exposed, Mao delivers an accurate portrait to the Mongolian Xiongnu khan, who threatens to invade China unless Zhaojun is given to him in marriage. Persuaded by his ministers, the love-struck emperor accedes after Zhaojun offers to sacrifice herself for peace.

Whereas in earlier versions of the legend Zhaojun marries the Xiongnu khan, in Ma's play she drowns herself at the border. In preserving her honor, the play registers more acute anxieties about miscegenation with foreigners. And by juxtaposing Mao's colloquial doggerel against the sympathetic characters' poetic language, the play also underscores class distinctions. For all his refinement, however, the emperor can only decry his helplessness. His despair culminates in the final arias, sung upon awakening from a dream in which a Xiongnu soldier tears away his beloved. Projecting his sadness onto a circling goose (who should be migrating south), the emperor hears its incessant cries as confirming the disorder afflicting nature's cycles. (The play's full title, *A Lone Goose Disturbs a Deep Dream in Autumn in the Han Palace,* situates his disorienting loss amid the orderly transience of seasons.) With large armies but lacking brave generals, surrounded by corrupt officials, the emperor laments, "Not seeing her flowering spirit, how can I enjoy the scenery of my gardens?"

Other Yuan dramas indict institutions of law and morality, suggesting that such systems may be more murderous than individuals. Guan Hanqing's 關漢卿 (ca. 1225–1302) *The Injustice Done to Dou E* 竇娥冤 dramatizes the tale of a wrongly executed young widow. The drama opens as an impoverished scholar, departing to take the examinations, betroths his seven-year-old daughter in repayment of a debt. Jumping ahead thirteen years, Dou E, already a widow at twenty, refuses to marry a man who has rescued her mother-in-law from murder. When the opportunistic suitor accidentally poisons his father, he frames Dou E for the death, and the innocent heroine, tortured by an uncaring court, confesses. Confident that heaven will protest the injustice of her beheading, Dou E predicts that three paranormal events will vindicate her. As portended, her blood travels up a white streamer (instead of dripping), snow falls in June, and a three-year drought afflicts the region. These outcomes, especially the famous "snow in June," render a sense of poetic justice further fulfilled when Dou E's father returns as a high official, convicts the wrongdoers, and clears his daughter's name. For an audience that values family reputation above individual life, this ending may vindicate Dou E's martyrdom. Yet the drama also conveys the tragic dimensions of malfeasance and injustice.

Dramatic romances

The Ming imperial court's sponsorship of operas led to longer dramatic romances and elaborate musical theater. More freewheeling than the northern variety plays, these dramas consist of 10 to 240 scenes (often 30 to 50) with large casts of singing characters. These operas are typically didactic melodramas about filial piety, separated lovers, mistaken identities, and belated reunions. Opening with a summary, they tend to feature obligatory scenes of love, battle, and comedy, as well as happy endings.

The masterpiece of Ming-era aristocratic theater is Tang Xianzu's 湯顯祖 (1550–1616) fifty-five-scene opera, *Peony Pavilion* 牡丹亭 (1598). Opening scenes dramatize the enlivening force of love, contrasting the young Liniang's endearing spring fever (stimulated by her study of the *Classic of Poetry*) with the repressed life of her tutor, a withered pedant deadened to both love and nature. After a dream encounter with a young lover in a garden pavilion, Liniang dies of lovesickness and, through another dream, pursues her passion from beyond the grave.

After the young Mengmei falls in love with Liniang's portrait, he encounters her ghostly apparition:

LIU MENGMEI (*enters*):

. . .

"Ever since I set eyes on the beauty in the portrait I've longed for her day and night. . . .

. . .

"Ah lady, lady, I die of longing for you!"

. . .

"Surely there must be a love affinity fated between this lady and myself?"

. . .

(*Sound of wind from offstage; his lamp flickers.*)

Suddenly a chill gust of wind. I must be careful . . .

After Liniang guides Mengmei to exhume and revivify her, her father imprisons him for robbing her tomb. Yet unlike the tragic *Romeo and Juliet* by Tang's English contemporary, *Peony Pavilion* grants love the power to overcome both mortality and conventional morality. By framing the lovers' transgressions as dreams, the lyrical romance subtly challenges convention and elevates erotic love, whose power of redemption is fully realized when the couple finally consummates their love as flesh-and-blood humans.

Barriers to passion become more intractable in Kong Shangren's 孔尚任 (1648–1718) highly literary *Peach Blossom Fan* 桃花扇

9. Still popular in China and abroad, this scene from the sixteenth-century *Peony Pavilion* **was staged by Ars Electronica Futurelab at the eARTS Festival Shanghai in 2007.**

(1699), a love story set amid the historical intrigues that hastened the collapse of the Ming dynasty. The doom-laden dramatic romance takes place in Nanjing, where the Ming court fled after rebels overran the north and the emperor committed suicide. Against a mercenary clique, the young hero, Hou Fangyu, joins with other loyalists to reform government corruption by promoting Confucian ideals.

The play's title refers to a fan that Fangyu gives to his beloved courtesan, Fragrant Princess, during a banquet celebrating their union. Upon learning that the banquet has been underwritten by a scheming court dramatist, the penurious Fangyu almost accepts, but Fragrant Princess righteously refuses the ill-gotten gifts. And after Fangyu leaves to join the army, the corrupt clique pressures Fragrant Princess to marry a high official.

When the villains try to abduct her, Fragrant Princess knocks her head against the floor and bloodies her fan. Illustrating the power of culture to prevail over violence, she sends Fangyu the fan with the bloodstains repainted into peach blossoms. Though the lovers meet again at a mourning ceremony for the last Ming emperor, hopes for a reunion are dashed when Chang, the Daoist overseeing the ceremony, objects to their selfish passion. Rather than betray the Ming court, they agree to withdraw into Daoist reclusion:

CHANG: For the male, let the south be his direction. Let Hou Fangyu depart for the southernmost hills, there to cultivate the Way.

HOU: I go. Understanding the Way, I perceive the depths of my folly. *(Ting leads Hou offstage.)*

CHANG: For the female, let her direction be the north. Let Fragrant Princess depart for the northernmost hills, there to cultivate the Way.

FRAGRANT PRINCESS: I go. All is illusion. . . .

"Promptbook" tales: crib sheets?

During the Song dynasty, the proliferation of professional storytellers led to the development of written vernacular tales. Often reworkings of tales of the marvelous, these expanded stories were intended for a wider audience. Characters include not only young scholars, beautiful courtesans, and corrupt officials but also crafty merchants, loyal servants, and wise monks. Ghosts also appear, although such supernatural elements generally serve the workings of this-worldly retribution.

Riding on the popularity of oral storytelling, these more consciously crafted narratives developed from the late thirteenth century. By the late sixteenth century, "spoken text" 話本 tales frequently borrowed storytelling's conventions and set phrases (e.g., "the tale divides into two directions" indicates a change of setting). Like a storyteller, the narrator often interrupts with couplets, poems, and moralizing asides. Unlike the poems attributed to characters in classical tales of the marvelous, poems in vernacular tales tend to reenact storytellers' opening prologues (allowing latecomers to hear the full main tale). Long believed to be scripts for such earlier oral tales, the "spoken text" genre has generally been translated as "promptbook." Yet since another term (底子) names storytellers' crib sheets, writers more likely invented the "spoken text" genre to sell to a growing reading public.

Reflecting the aspirations of the newly rising middle class, these stories told of class mobility for enterprising commoners, virtuous courtesans, and other sincere seekers of happiness. The possibility of women's empowerment is found in some unlikely settings. In one story, a garrulous young woman tells her parents-in-law to annul her marriage if they don't like her mouthing off, and then leaves to become a nun. Another story tells of a barren couple who take in a blind old woman and then conceive a daughter upon her death. Sharing many affinities with her earlier incarnation, the daughter's independence from the "world of dust" is confirmed when she disappears from her bridal carriage rather than enter into marriage.

The sense of wonder in such stories is captured in the titles of the most famous anthologies, including *Lasting Words to Awaken the World* 醒世恆言 (1627), one of three collections edited by Feng Menglong 馮夢龍 (1574–1646), and Ling Mengchu's 凌濛初 (1580–1644) two-volume *Pounding the Table in Amazement* 拍案驚奇 (1628 and 1632). Like many tales in the literary language, these vernacular stories usually emphasize reward for virtue and retribution for moral transgressions. But they also show sympathy for human frailties and the compromises people make to adapt to their predicaments.

An exemplar of a self-determining woman is found in "The Oil Peddler Courts the Courtesan" 賣油郎獨佔花魁 from Feng's *Lasting Words* collection. Following opening accounts of the protagonists' harrowing backstories, the action rises when the industrious Qinzhong, selling lamp oil door-to-door, first glimpses the beautiful Meiniang, the capital's most coveted courtesan. For more than a year he scrimps and saves to buy a night with her; and although she arrives late, drinks too much, and quickly falls asleep exhausted, his joy is hardly diminished. When she awakes only to retch, he catches her vomit in his sleeve, serves her tea, and chastely holds her as she falls back to sleep. In the morning, she recalls his kindness and realizes the purity of his love for her: "Such a good man is hard to find! So loyal and honest, sensible yet sensitive, hiding my faults and praising my virtues. Not one in a hundred thousand could match him. Such a pity he's just a merchant; were he a gentleman, I'd gladly give myself to him." Moved by his continuing acts of devotion, Meiniang resolves to transform her life. Though once a child refugee sold into an elite brothel and groomed to be a plaything of the rich and famous, the resourceful courtesan has covertly saved a small fortune. After buying her freedom, she marries the humble oil peddler and bankrolls his small business. Diligently building on her capital, the commoner couple prospers, begets scholars, and practices philanthropy.

Novels-in-chapters

As with vernacular stories, the Ming-era rise of long "fiction-in-chapters" 章回小說 owed much to oral storytelling. (The term "chapter" 章回 probably referred to a "session" 回.) Whereas shorter vernacular fiction tends to emphasize plot and character, longer works often evoke lyrical grand visions. For example, many novels present neo-Confucian ideals of a patterned moral universe governed by a natural Way, ideals that helped re-Sinify China after the Mongol Yuan dynasty.

At the same time, these novels' realism about human diversity raises doubts about the chances of reconciling conflicting values in a world sullied by greed and lust. Many of these novels revel in, yet seek to transcend, what Buddhists call the "world of dust." In their gritty portrayals of rebels, bandits, and other defiers of moral order, some readers see heroes, but others see efforts to contain subversive ideas and marginal groups, including women.

Scholars sometimes liken traditional novels to Chinese gardens and landscape painting, both of which encourage wandering rather than a single fixed perspective or presentation. Seasonal, geographic, or mythic patterns commonly structure episodic plots, often of a hundred or more chapters. Chapters usually end with invitations to continue ("If you want to know what happens, just listen to the next chapter"), but such dovetailing does not guarantee a larger architecture. Following conventions from drama, many novels climax about two-thirds of the way through, leaving a long denouement and a sense of life's continuation.

The four masterworks of the Ming dynasty

Depicting the Han dynasty's fall and the rise of three warring kingdoms (early third century), the *Romance of the Three Kingdoms* 三國志演義 enacts material from historical sources. (The term translated here as "romance," *yanyi* 演義, literally means "elaboration of meaning.") Beginning as a fourteenth-century manuscript, the novel, first published in 1522, was revised by generations of writer-editors and is most commonly read in Mao Zonggang's 毛宗崗 (1632–1709) version with commentary (1679). The novel has inspired elaborate filmic adaptations, including CCTV's 1994 blockbuster series of eighty-four, hour-long episodes. The television series was China's most costly to date, featured a cast of 400,000 and drew a record audience of 1.2 billion viewers worldwide.

Mixing simple classical narration with more colloquial dialogue, the novel's 120 chapters give it epic length and feel. By integrating so much popular history into one long saga, the novel reinforces the notion that history follows larger patterns. Individuals, the plot implies, exercise but limited power within the workings of history's moral order, a perspective articulated in Mao Zonggang's preface: "Under heaven, grand affairs long divided must be reunited, and those long united must divide."

In dramatizing historical events, the novel nonetheless powerfully depicts the characters' personal struggles, making its heroes oft invoked archetypes for commentary about intrigue, villainy, and politics. Against the moody, ruthless poet-ruler Cao Cao, king of Wei, the novel pits Liu Bei, king of Shu-Han, and his two sworn brothers, the courageous but conceited general Guan Yu and the imperious and short-tempered Zhang Fei. Their ill-fated dream of reunifying the empire gains strength when Liu recruits the Daoist sage Zhuge Liang. At the decisive Battle at Red Cliffs, Zhuge summons southeastern winds to fan fires that rout Cao Cao's forces, a victory sealing the tripartition of the country.

Though the novel presents Liu as the rightful heir to restore a united Han empire, his personal loyalties make him vulnerable to headstrong decisions. And because Zhuge must bow to Liu's choices, his resourcefulness has limited effect. For all his Confucian loyalty, Zhuge cannot dissuade Liu from pursuing personal revenge. And despite Zhuge's scruples about commitment, after Liu's blind vengeance results in his own death and the kingdom is clearly lost, Zhuge faithfully serves Liu's feckless son.

The novel's emphasis on moral retribution may reinforce beliefs in historical cycles, but the upshot is less clear. Does the novel suggest that though it may take centuries, cycles of union and disunion will ultimately restore virtuous rulers? Or might the novel's portrayal of history's cycles shed irony on ideals of dynastic order? As a famous line from the novel reminds us, "The pursuit of goals lies in humans, but accomplishment lies with heaven."

A second Ming masterpiece, *Water Margin* 水滸傳 (a.k.a. *Outlaws of the Marsh,* ca. 1550) portrays a gang of 108 hard-drinking, audacious bandits from the early twelfth century. The thirty-six main heroes come from all walks of life, driven to banditry by indignation over government corruption, vengeance, coercion by other outlaws, or in the case of the generous yet ruthless leader Song Jiang, a wife's betrayal. Rich in realistic details of martial arts, claims of friendship, and appetites, the novel climaxes with a grand banquet when the band reaches the preordained number of 108 (including three women). In the name of righteousness, these loyal outlaws steal from the wealthy, defeat government troops, negotiate their own amnesty, and then defend the Song dynasty against rebels. But they show innocent children and women no mercy, and graphic descriptions of massacres, flaying, and cannibalism have led some scholars to decry the heroes' sadism. Gang mentality rules, enforced by a harsh code based above all on revenge and misogyny. Hating women for their weakness and lust, the bandits view sexual abstinence as a sign of machismo, and the killing of women for adultery as a sign of brotherhood.

More thoroughly colloquial than *Romance of the Three Kingdoms, Water Margin*'s heavy use of stock phrases and popular songs made the novel accessible to more readers, and raised the stakes for commentators seeking to control the novel's social effects. Readers debate whether the novel celebrates peasant rebellion, or offers a cautionary fable about the sinister terror of gang mentality. (Since multiple authors and editors crafted the novel, it may not have a consistent ideology.) Even if they idolize the novel's rebellious adventurers, it is hard for readers not to come away chastened by the destruction and chaos that ensue when vengeance is untempered by Confucian morals.

Such novels evolved through processes of accretion, and, as with the rewriting of poems, scholars often appropriated earlier versions for ideological purposes. To enhance both didactic and commercial value, major novels were typically published with "how to read" essays and interlinear, marginal, and chapter commentaries that tended to impose Confucian interpretations. (When necessary, inconsistencies would be explained as hints to read more carefully.) Highlighting natural patterns, ethical acts and consequences, and the workings of retribution, critics and editors also addressed Buddhist and Daoist themes, as well as strengths and weaknesses of structure, style, and pacing.

By treating fiction as serious literature worthy of exegesis, these commentaries radically expanded the scope of literary theory, previously devoted almost exclusively to poetry. Some editors also substantially altered their material, as Jin Shengtan 金聖嘆 (1608–61) did in abridging a 120-chapter version of *Water Margin* to 70 chapters (1641). Divergent commentaries led to serious debates, as in the case of *Romance of the Three Kingdoms*. Whereas some interpret the novel's portrayal of bravery and loyalty as promoting these cherished Ming values, others see the characters' fateful overconfidence as subtly critiquing Ming imperial propaganda.

Possibly the most retold East Asian classic, *Journey to the West* 西遊記 (1592) satirizes social ills through recrafting the tale of the historical monk Xuanzang's (596–664) perilous pilgrimage to India. Developed out of the monk's travelogue, biographies, prosimetric legends, and dramas, the hundred-chapter adventure novel (possibly by Wu Cheng'en 吳承恩, ca. 1500–82) is nonetheless more unified than earlier novels. Abandoned in infancy after a bandit abducts and rapes his widowed mother, the Xuanzang of the novel is plagued by fears and anxieties. But he ultimately triumphs, bringing back and translating three canons of Buddhist sutras (the "Three Baskets" of his other name, Tripitaka).

The picaresque novel endows the dutiful but apprehensive monk with four superhuman companions: a clever but impetuous monkey, a lustful pig, a "Sand Monk," and a white horse. Most important is Monkey, whose full name means "the Monkey Awakened to Emptiness," and whose early life opens the novel. Clever and resourceful, he is, like the human mind, wild and restless until controlled through Buddhist discipline. A popular hero later reincarnated in countless cartoons, films, television series, and video games, Monkey frequently rescues the group with his magical transforming rod. Yet his ill-focused energies risk everyone's safety but for Xuanzang's control.

Read as allegory, Xuanzang is a spiritual seeker, Monkey his heart-mind, the white horse his will, Pigsy his bodily desires, and Sand Monk his connection to the earth. The journey represents the cultivation of the heart-mind, and the novel's perils and monsters stand for distortions that obscure the path to Enlightenment. Scholars debate the degree of irony in the novel's presentation of spiritual quest. Is it an epic or a mock-epic? Does it champion Buddhist salvation or advocate for synthesizing Confucian, Daoist, and Buddhist beliefs?

Numerous sequels and midquels added to the novel's influence and fame. Like its parent novel, *Supplement to Journey to the West* 西遊補 (1641) offers a trenchant social satire combined with a masterful Buddhist allegory about the ways passions (情 *qing*) can imprison the heart. Ensnarled by Mackerel (鯖 *qing*, a homophone for passion) in a series of hallucinations, Monkey broadens his perspective to see the nature of desire, its delusions, and his own conditioned tendencies. As he does, the point of view shifts from his perspective to more omniscient narration, just one of several consciously crafted literary techniques. Short by the standards of the time, this sixteen-chapter midquel features a Tower of Myriad Mirrors, a group of space-walkers chiseling a hole in the firmament, and other surreal elements that make the novel ripe for psychoanalytic readings as dreamwork on anxiety.

Another supplement, the *Later Journey to the West* 後西遊記 (1715) tells of the heroes' pilgrimage to a mountain with seventy-two pits of demons' temptations, all ultimately related to the seven emotions and six desires. (Pigsy falls prey to flattery, and Monkey to ambition.)

The last of the four Ming-dynasty masterpieces, *The Plum in the Golden Vase* 金瓶梅 (literally *Gold, Vase, Plum*, 1618), notorious for its sexual passages, colorfully portrays a community obsessed with money, status, and sensual indulgence. One of the earliest novels of manners, its attention to social settings, roles, and expectations shows how class mores and conditioning determine individual feelings and behaviors. Within the novel's hundred chapters, six wives compete for the attentions of the unscrupulous drug merchant and influence peddler Ximen Qing. The novel borrows its setting, Qing, his concubine Golden Lotus, and several other characters from an episode in *Water Margin*, but its parody frees the novel from the mythic frameworks that characterize that work, *Three Kingdoms*, and *Journey*. Now desire itself motivates the action. And though set in the twelfth century, the domestic drama is situated within an exhaustively detailed sixteenth-century milieu.

By delaying the bandit Wu Song's revenge against his adulterous sister-in-law and her lover for murdering his elder brother, the novel allows Qing to sow the seeds of his own destruction. (Legend has it that a traditionalist author wrote the novel to pursue a vendetta against the corrupt son of the man who executed his father.) After Qing's affair with his neighbor Ping'er (the Vase of the title) results in her husband's death, Qing combines their properties to construct an ostentatious garden to showcase his wealth and station. Though Qing is himself functionally illiterate, his garden "study" has all the trappings of literati culture. Yet his indiscriminate display of overnumerous paintings betrays his poor taste, and the political machinations and debauchery that ensue there reveal his philistine pretensions. After Ping'er becomes

Qing's clear favorite, the resentful Lotus spies on them copulating in a garden pavilion and learns of Ping'er's pregnancy. Later that day Qing uses Lotus's footbindings to spread-eagle her in the garden's notorious grape arbor, then inebriates and ravishes her, and the chastened Lotus returns to her room with just one of her slippers.

Though less focused on explicit sex than Li Yu's 李漁 (1611–80) comic-erotic *The Carnal Prayer Mat* 肉蒲團 (1657), the novel's graphic sadomasochistic passages explore lust's power to corrupt, the insatiability of desire, and the pain of power exchanges. After the jealous Lotus causes the death of Ping'er's son, and Ping'er dies of grief, Lotus uses aphrodisiacs from an Indian monk to lure Qing to die through sexual overexertion. "Be judicious in your use of these remedies," the monk counsels Qing, but this caution only piques Qing's licentiousness. After Qing's excesses precipitate his death, his entourage of manipulative social climbers can do little but eulogize their departed patron, and his son by his principal wife, born at the moment of his death, becomes a monk.

For many commentators, these workings of retribution offer sustained lessons in Buddhist and Confucian ethics. For some, the novel's juxtapositions of heterogeneous elements (earlier songs, Buddhist stories, dramas, and novels) result in ironic moral critique. Following the model of the Confucian *Great Learning*, Qing's moral failings not only sow disorder in his household but also contribute to larger social decline and the dynasty's political collapse. Commentators often attribute such a coherent design to a single author, although it might also result from plural authorship. And what may be ironic distance on the characters' stereotypical worldviews might protest rather than uphold Confucian practices.

Though many modern leftist scholars claim that such vernacular works reflected the masses, most of the best fiction was *literati* fiction. From the seventeenth century on, novels tended to rewrite, parody, and subvert earlier works in a kind of literary game.

Keeping in mind their authors' prestige may lead to different conclusions about whether these texts ultimately legitimatize or critique prevailing political and social conditions.

Eighteenth-century satire

Obsession with status also dominates Wu Jingzi's 吳敬梓 (1701–54) *The Unofficial History of the Forest of Scholars* 儒林外史 (1750). Skeptical about the efficacy of moral ideals, especially when pursued too rigidly, Wu's "outer history" parodies official biographies by lampooning the mostly petty preoccupations of roughly seventy literati. Even though an opening poem decries the vanity of "success, fame, riches, and rank," most of the characters either shamelessly pursue wealth and status through conventional channels or forsake bureaucratic careers for equally dubious motives.

To mask insecurities, even characters who reject the examination system seek personal validation, and the novel's trenchant satire voices a sense of cultural crisis. Unlike earlier novels that label characters upon their first appearance, *The Scholars* reveals the characters' personalities through their actions, a panoply of practices for accumulating cultural capital: success in the civil service exams, association with degree holders, marriage alliances, publishing model exam essays, and even impersonation. As Wu's semi-autobiographical agonist, Du Shaoqing, squanders his inheritance on indiscriminate grand acts, he is just one of the anti-establishment eccentrics who purchase status by sponsoring lavish events, from a beauty contest for female impersonators to a temple dedication honoring an ancient Confucian sage. The latter ritual, the novel's putative climax, results in little but nostalgia. Each participant subsequently fails in his attempts to restore moral order, and the temple is later discovered in ruins, the dusty ceremony program now illegible. Recalling the final memorial service in *Peach Blossom Fan*, Du's fruitless ceremony might also be a veiled allegory protesting the Manchu dynasty.

For some readers, this "literati novel" consoles by its presentation of upright characters devoted to moral cultivation through classical study, the arts, and ritual practices. Central to this interpretation is the opening chapter's idealized portrayal of the painter Wang Mian (the only historical character) and the final chapter's account of four humble literati. Recalling the virtuous Wang, who construes a hundred small falling stars as a sign of heaven's pity "to maintain the literary tradition," the four practitioners of the zither, chess, calligraphy, and painting—unsullied by bureaucratic pursuits of fame—serve as foils against other characters' mercenary utilitarianism. Yet the novel's exposure of hypocrisy might undercut as easily as champion the nobility of the scholarly tradition, especially given its unprecedented verisimilitude. (Full of essayistic digressions, but with less reliance on stock phrases and preexisting materials, the novel employs a more consistent vernacular style.)

Dream of the Red Chamber

Dream of the Red Chamber 紅樓夢 (1792), with more than 100 million copies sold, ranks among the world's top five all-time bestselling novels (and among the top fifteen bestselling books, including the Bible and the Qur'ān). Also known as *Story of the Stone* (the title of the novel's most elegant English translation), the novel opens with a mythic account of the story's origin. A divine stone-in-waiting, left unused after the repair of the heavens, is reincarnated into the wealthy Jia family. Born with a piece of jade in his mouth and a consuming need to love and be loved, Baoyu (Precious Jade) shares a predestined association with his cousin Daiyu. She owes him a cosmic debt because when he was a stone and she a flower in their prior existence, he awoke her to sentience by watering her with dew. Determined to return his kindness, the flower-turned-fairygirl had resolved to repay his sweet dew with a lifetime of human tears.

In one of the novel's most vivid scenes, Baoyu finds Daiyu burying fallen flowers to protect them from trampling. "I have a flower grave in that corner. Today I'll sweep all the petals into this silk bag and bury them. With time they'll rejoin the earth." When Baoyu offers to put down his book to help, Daiyu demands to see what he's reading. The book turns out to be *Story of the Western Wing*, and Daiyu later recalls the lament of the lovelorn Yingying:

> As flowers fall and the flowing stream runs red,
> A thousand sickly fancies crowd the mind.

Since she was a flower in her previous incarnation, the sensitive Daiyu is, on a mythic level, also burying herself. Plagued by worry that Baoyu will marry someone else, she withers away, and her frailty contributes to the outcome she most fears. After the family betroths Baoyu to another cousin and Daiyu's melancholy leads to her death, the flowers' burial becomes more poignant. Symbols of neglected beauty, the flowers also connect Daiyu to Yingying, the heroine of the play Baoyu shared with her.

For some, the novel's main theme is the conflict between Baoyu's desire for liberation from suffering and his passionate emotional attachment to his female companions. Though the Daoist-Buddhist ideal of liberation ultimately prevails when Baoyu leaves to become a monk, many voices in the novel defend attachment as the essence of human-heartedness. The novel's many poems, dramas, and riddles also belie its message of detachment. For although literary works may reveal the vanities of the world of red dust, they also testify to the potential for creativity to influence karmic destiny.

Ultimately, *Dream* suggests the inadequacy of prevalent conceptions of love. The tragic disappointments facing the young lovers and their families point to the compromises of arranged marriage, but also to the dreamlike nature of love itself. So real during the dream, and so vital that the characters long to make it permanent, love turns out to be ephemeral.

Along these lines, numerous formal elements reinforce the novel's inquiry into reality and illusion. Early in the novel a poem cycle foretells the fates of Baoyu's closest female companions, destinies that unfold in the last forty chapters. As such poems and symbols foreshadow Baoyu's withdrawal from the mundane world as well as impending tragedy for the Jia family, word plays, pairs of symbolic twins, and other structuring details further suggest a cosmic order beyond human comprehension or control. (The surname Jia, a homophone for "false," is mirrored by a family surnamed Zhen, a homophone for "true.") Amid the novel's multiple themes, doubling devices, and *mises en abyme,* the story's many mirrors invoke an ideal of clear reflection and the power of mimetic knowledge.

Dream also further riddles the porous boundary between fiction and commentary. Cao Xueqin 曹雪芹 (1715–63), the scion of an elite family in decline, wrote the first eighty chapters; after Cao's death an editor completed the 120-chapter version read today. As different versions with commentaries circulated in manuscript before the novel's publication, fierce debates arose about Cao's purported revisions, many of which left inconsistencies in the text.

These debates have spawned a cottage industry of "Red-ology" devoted to questions of authorship, editions, and hidden meanings. Some scholars interpret the novel as an attack on the decadence of feudal society. For them, the Jia family's fated decline is consonant with a cyclic view of Chinese dynasties, whereby the powerful fall because of moral dissolution and the resultant withdrawal of heaven's mandate. This historical dimension lends a larger significance to allegedly autobiographical elements. What is at stake in the novel is not just individual loss but the entire elite traditional heritage.

As much as the novel paints the folly and corruption bred by elite privilege, it is also one of the world's most moving testimonies to the beauty of literary culture. Countless readers of *Dream* have learned about love and longing, identified with its protagonists, and found consolation when facing their own losses in love. The novel inspired more than thirty sequels, including one by the Manchu poet Gu Taiqing 顧太清 (1799–1876). Gu's *Shadows of Dream of the Red Chamber* 紅樓夢影, probably first published posthumously in 1877, may be China's earliest surviving novel by a woman.

If you want to know how the wars and tumult of the nineteenth and twentieth centuries would reorder perspectives on human aspirations, just turn to the next chapter!

Chapter 5
Modern literature: trauma, movements, and bus stops

In Gao Xingjian's 高行健 (1940-) play *Bus Stop* 車站 (1983), eight characters, stuck in an outer suburb, wait for a bus. Though sound effects announce passing buses, none stops, and the characters gradually despair of ever reaching the city. Gramps cannot get to his chess match; Girl misses her date; and Hothead fears losing his chance to taste yogurt. Mom tries to teach Hothead some manners, consoles the lovelorn girl, and worries about her husband and child, whose laundry awaits her weekend visits. Early on, without explanation, the Silent Person leaves to walk, and when the others realize that ten years have passed, they regret not having followed his example.

At regular intervals, the audience sees the silhouetted Silent Person walking, accompanied by a signature tune. His movement serves as a foil for the waiting characters, whose predicament recalls that of Vladimir and Estragon in Samuel Beckett's *Waiting for Godot* (1953). Drawing on both traditional Chinese theater (with its interplay of sound and drama) and French theater of the absurd, Gao's characters sometimes talk for the sake of talking. But their dialogues also express deep longings and trenchant social criticisms. For Glasses, who misses his final chance to take the College Entrance Exam, the waiting becomes unbearable: "Life has left us behind. The world has forgotten us. A lifespan passes by in vain right before your eyes." "Waiting's not so bad," the master carpenter counters later, when the actors break character to deliver overlapping lines. "People wait because they have hope."

A political allegory of China's passage from the countryside to the city, Gao's play suggests five themes central to the modernization and globalization of Chinese literature. Though many critics interpret the play as signaling the government's failure to deliver the means of progress, others hear in it ongoing commitments to national pride, humanism, progress, memory, and pleasure. Although such positive aspirations have often been downplayed by critics of Gao's 2000 Nobel Prize in Literature, their resonance for the Nobel Committee and for his other admirers suggests these themes' centrality in contemporary world literature.

Pursuing the nation

After Gao's characters have waited a year, they try to block the road as a bus approaches. It blares its horn, and the characters scatter as the bus, full of foreigners, speeds past. It was a tourist bus for foreigners, Mom explains, which would have required foreign currency certificates. This affront further discourages them, and a little later Glasses despairs that no bus will come: "Let's walk, as that guy did. In the time we've spent foolishly waiting at this bus stop, someone could have not only arrived in the city, but accomplished something there. What are we waiting for?"

Because the characters decide to set off on foot only at the end of the play, their passivity has also been interpreted as an allegory for China's belated modernization. Though many features of modern societies were developing in China by at least the sixteenth century, China was militarily unprepared when European powers forcibly entered China in the nineteenth century. After disputes over Britain's importation of opium led to the Opium Wars, a series of unequal treaties imposed mercantilism (what would now be called free trade), opened China's ports, created foreign concessions in key cities, and made Hong Kong a British colony.

Concerned that China would be carved up like a melon, reformers pursued a limited Westernization movement—based on the notion of "Chinese essence, Western means"—until Japan too defeated China in the 1894–95 war over Korea. After Japan imposed its own unequal treaty that, among other humiliations, made the island of Taiwan a Japanese colony, many Chinese saw Japan's power as the result of the Meiji regime's embrace of Westernization. As Yan Fu 嚴復 (1853–1921) and others translated works by thinkers such as Thomas Huxley, Herbert Spencer, Adam Smith, John Stuart Mill, and Montesquieu, "survival of the fittest" and other vocabulary from the social sciences increasingly shaped Chinese intellectuals' understanding of their nation's dilemmas, and they advocated a more radical modernization program for China.

This nationalistic project supported Chinese literature's evolution into a distinct and respected field. Convinced that China's survival depended on an educated citizenry, reformers published vernacular novels, newspapers, and magazines. From Beijing University's founding in 1898, newly established universities nurtured academic study of the humanities, including Chinese and foreign literatures, and literary groups formed around key universities. With the abolition of the civil service exams in 1905, intellectuals gained further independence from the government.

To buttress the newly reconceived nation, reformers drew heavily on ideas and forms in Western literature, available thanks to, among others, Lin Shu's 林紓 (1852–1924) translations of more than a hundred novels by writers including Conan Doyle, Sir Walter Scott, Dickens, Balzac, and Tolstoy. Crediting Western novels for the steady progress of Europe, America, and Japan, the reformer Liang Qichao 梁啟超 (1873–1929) published numerous Western works in his journal, *New Fiction* 新小說 (1902–6), and in 1902 Liang explicitly called for a transformation of China's own fiction: "If one intends to renovate the people of a nation, one must first renovate its fiction."

These concerns intensified after a series of uprisings overturned the Qing dynasty in 1911. The new Republic of China (1912–) seemed ill equipped to address the nation's troubles, and the revolution of 1911 came to be seen as a "revolution betrayed" after the Republic's first president tried to declare himself emperor. Warlords controlled much of China until the National Revolutionary Army, led by General Chiang Kai-shek 蔣介石 (1887–1975), reunited the country through the Northern Expedition (1926–28).

During this period, journals such as *New Youth* 新青年 (1915–26) criticized the patriarchal family system and other Confucian "feudal" traditions they deemed responsible for the nation's weaknesses. Eager to orient China toward the future, intellectuals launched a New Culture Movement championing individual freedom, feminism, democracy, science, and a more accessible vernacular literature. This movement, sometimes called the Chinese "Enlightenment," became politicized once students at Beijing University launched their own journal, *New Tide* 新潮 (1919–22), and demonstrated to protest the Allies' plan to give Germany's territories in China to Japan at the Paris Peace Conference. These demonstrations, which began on May 4, 1919, brought democratic and nationalist ideals to a larger popular base and led many in this "May Fourth Movement" to turn to the Left and found the Chinese Communist Party (CCP) in 1921.

As foreign powers' designs on China made urgent the task of modernizing its citizens, many reformers believed that depictions of individual consciousness were key to this modernization. Self-expression gained prominence in novels, stories, plays, and poems, but such individualism was deeply rooted in social responsibility and what critic C. T. Hsia later called modern Chinese literature's "obsession with China."

Even writers committed to European romanticism and "art for art's sake" felt deep concern for China's standing. In the semi-autobiographical story "Sinking" 沈淪 (1921), Yu Dafu's 郁達夫 (1896–1945) protagonist, feeling "maltreated by the world," ties his personal despair to China's national destiny: "China, ah China! How can you not rise up wealthy and strong? I can no longer go on secretly suffering!" And in "Dead Water" 死水 (1926), the poet Wen Yiduo 聞一多 (1899–1946), an ardent champion of poetry's musical, pictorial, and architectural beauty, closes with an ominous metaphor for his country—especially eerie in light of Wen's later assassination by Nationalist agents.

> Here is a ditch of hopelessly dead water—
> a region where beauty can never reside.
> Might as well let the devil cultivate it—
> and see what sort of world it can provide.

Expressions of nationalism proliferated in works of leftist writers such as Wu Zuxiang 吳祖湘 (1908–94). In Wu's satirical "Young Master Gets His Tonic" 官官的補品 (1932), the spoiled young narrator bolsters his health with milk expressed by a wet nurse, from whose husband he had earlier purchased blood, and marvels with self-satisfaction: "What a wonderful world it is; if you have the money, there's nothing you can't buy." Oblivious as the narrator is to the economic and political structures that support his indolence, he reports his cousin's pointed analysis:

> Everything around here going downhill from one day to the next
> has nothing to do with fate. If you ask me, it's because we've been
> cheated out of all our money by the foreigners. . . . All these things
> are foreign invented, foreign manufactured, ways they've thought up
> to cheat us Chinese out of our money; . . . how are you going to stop
> the country from getting poorer? And then you talk about fate!

Issues of national identity also mark literature on Taiwan, especially in works reflecting on the period of Japanese Colonialism (1895–1945). In "The Doctor's Mother" 先生媽 (1945), Wu Zhuoliu 吳濁流 (1900–76) documents the suppression of

Taiwanese identity through his mocking portrayal of a doctor's obsessive pursuit of status. The doctor takes a Japanese name, entertains Japanese officials, and otherwise creates a "Japanese-only household." His Taiwanese mother rejects his endeavor, slices up her kimono with a cleaver, and gives alms to beggars. Her stubbornness further alienates her family, but her philanthropy is rewarded on her deathbed, when an old beggar brings her favorite fried doughsticks; he is the only true mourner at her Japanese-style funeral.

Though Taiwan was returned to the Republic of China in 1945, the province separated politically from the mainland after the CCP won a bloody civil war (1946–49) and founded the People's Republic of China (PRC). After the Nationalist Party (GMD) fled to Taiwan during what they called the Communist "takeover" of the mainland, intellectuals on Taiwan deemed themselves the guardians of traditional Chinese culture. Reinforcing the GMD's campaign to restore the lost homeland, nostalgic anti-Communist fiction condemned the CCP not only for China's political crisis but for threatening the survival of China's ethical tradition.

The most probing of Taiwan's anti-Communist historical novels may be Jiang Gui's 姜貴 (1908–80) *Rival Suns* 重陽 (1961), set in Shanghai and Wuhan from 1923 to 1927, the year of the CCP-GMD split. Ambitious but without means, Hong Tongye serves a French family that represents two faces of Western imperialism: Mr. Lefebvre is an arms dealer trafficking in drugs, his wife a proselytizing Christian. But as the disillusioned Tongye becomes involved with the Communist Liu Shaoqiao, the novel focuses on the reformers' hypocrisy in touting liberation while committing atrocities. When Tongye invokes the prospect of building a new society to justify deserting his indigent, bedridden mother, his sister questions, "If we can't even take care of our own mother, can we be qualified to worry about so many people's troubles?" Moreover, as Tongye abets Shaoqiao in acts of sexual torture, their relationship (possibly also sexual) could symbolize the

CCP-GMD alliance, and the novel suggests that the Nationalists' corruption and acquiescence to foreign imperialism facilitated the Communist victory.

Pursuing humanity

Although Gao's *Bus Stop* shares features with avant-garde theater, its realistic details follow in modern Chinese literature's dominant mode of critical realism. Mom can't live with her husband and child because she lacks the connections needed to have her work unit transferred to the city, and Gramps scolds Director Ma, director of a general store, for exchanging brand-name cigarettes for favors. At first Director Ma flaunts his privilege, and he cares little about missing a chance to be wined and dined, but he becomes more determined to reach the city as his indignation grows.

> DIRECTOR MA: I'm going. I have to get to the city to denounce the bus company. I'll track down the manager and ask him whom they're driving the buses for anyway. Is it for their own convenience or for us passengers? They have to take some responsibility! I'll take them to court and sue for compensation for the loss of our years as well as our health!

Gao's use of characters representing typical social roles recalls the stock characters of traditional Chinese drama. But his realism has more in common with the Norwegian playwright Henrik Ibsen, whose dramas, especially *A Doll's House* (1879), greatly influenced the new genre of modern Chinese "spoken drama." Ibsen's heroine Nora became a *cause célèbre* among intellectuals sympathetic to the New Culture Movement's advocacy of women's freedom. "What Happens When Nora Leaves Home?" 娜拉走後怎樣? asked Lu Xun 魯迅 (1881–1936) in a famous 1923 speech and essay by that title.

Often considered the vanguard of modern Chinese fiction, Lu Xun's stories helped launch the New Literature Movement.

Already by the late Qing period, "denunciation novels" documented corruption and inhumanity, but now writers made it their mission to criticize superstition, class inequality, and the exploitation of women. Condemning traditional classical-language literature as a reflection of feudalism, reformers drew on both imperial-era vernacular literature and Western languages to develop a modern written language. Much closer to speech (and thus called *baihua* 白話, "plain speech"), this language formed the basis of Standard Written Chinese and facilitated literature's service to social transformation.

Lu Xun's "A Madman's Diary" 狂人日記 (1918) cries out against exploitation in a hallucinatory modernist mode. After an opening preface written in classical Chinese, the story switches to *baihua* to present excerpts from a diary whose author, the preface explains, eventually recovered and presumably disowned the diary's insights. Yet even as details of his hysteria and delusions suggest the diarist's derangement, with his realization that classical texts conceal veiled exhortations to "eat people," he positions himself as the sole "real person" among wolves: "You should change, change from the bottom of your hearts. You must realize that there will be no place for man-eaters in the world of the future." The diary ends with a portentous call to "Save the children" followed by an ellipsis that may undermine the preface's claim about the madman's "recovery."

Stories such as "Madman's Diary" include modernist elements, but most "New Literature Movement" works employ straightforward realism to depict the suffering caused by the patriarchal family system, poverty, and other injustices. Many works appeal for compassion, as does Lu Xun's portrayal of an out-of-work scholar in "Kong Yiji" 孔乙己 (1919). Disenfranchised by his impractical classical education and taunted for the pilfering on which he survives, Kong is finally seen crawling, his legs broken for stealing. Just as the crippled Kong represents a class disabled by outmoded traditions, the story's uncaring child narrator represents the indifference Lu Xun most feared. In Ye Shaojun's 葉紹鈞 (1894–1988) "A Posthumous Son" 遺腹子 (1926), a loving couple, obsessed with having a son, bears seven daughters before a tiny son fails to survive. Foreshadowing the husband's suicide, the story indicts tradition as the source of his despair: "Along life's highway a poisoned arrow of tradition had cruelly pierced his heart." Yet the cycle continues. Three years later, as the devastated widow still imagines that she is pregnant, matchmakers arrive to arrange marriages for her eldest daughters.

From the story of a woman's sale by her husband in Xu Dishan's 許地山 (1893–1941) "The Merchant's Wife" 商人婦 (1921), to the dehumanizing rural poverty in Xiao Hong's 蕭紅 (1911–42) *The Field of Life and Death* 生死場 (1934), many works of the twenties and thirties present individuals whose determination and hard work cannot surmount the economic and social obstacles they face. In Lao She's 老舍 (1899–1966) depiction of Beijing's urban poor in *Rickshaw Boy* 駱駝祥子 (1937), a young rickshaw puller's aspirations and integrity cannot withstand the competition and other trials he suffers: from thefts and his wife's death in childbirth to a beloved's suicide and the climactic public execution of a union organizer he himself betrayed.

Leftist fiction and drama often depicted the dangers as well as the promises of abstract humanist ideals. In Ba Jin's 巴金 (1904–2005) passionate *Family* 家 (1931), the idealistic young writer Juehui confronts the feudal family system. Yet he colludes with the hierarchy he abhors when his political activism leads him to ignore the bondmaid who loves him, and who drowns herself rather than be made an elderly man's concubine. Ba's masterful *Ward Four* 第四病室 (1946) describes the desperate conditions of a wartime hospital, an allegory for the treatment of the poor more generally. In *Cold Nights* 寒夜 (1947), the most powerful of Ba's twenty novels, a common-law wife abandons her tubercular husband to pursue personal happiness and career fulfillment.

Writers on Taiwan, too, pursued liberal humanist themes, particularly during Taiwan's long decades of martial law (1949–87). As U.S. military and economic support promoted Western literature and philosophy, Western-influenced modernists treated themes of exile, alienation, and generational conflict. Other writers, resisting Taiwan's embrace of American capitalism and culture, responded with a vibrant "nativist literature," from Huang Chunming's 黄春明 (1939–) riveting account of a poor father's demeaning work as a clown advertisement in "His Son's Big Doll" 兒子的大玩偶 (1967) to Chen Yingzhen's 陳映真 (1937–) fifteen volumes of deeply moralistic works.

In Chen's "Roses in June" 六月裡的玫瑰花 (1967), Barney, a black American GI on R&R in Taiwan, falls in love with Emmy, a bargirl. Yet Emmy starts to remind Barney of a little girl he murdered in Vietnam, and also of his mother, who too worked as a prostitute for white men. As the trauma re-stimulates memories of his father beating his mother after she'd turned tricks to feed the family, Barney lands in a mental hospital, where Emmy sends him a rose every day. The story ends when the pregnant Emmy receives an official letter from the U.S. Army, a sign to the reader that Barney has honored his promise to marry her. Yet the story's final paragraph shatters Emmy's illusion that it announces a promotion; Barney has died for his country. While most of Taiwan supported what the Vietnamese call "the American War," Chen's story ventures dissident opposition, possibly a reason for which Chen was imprisoned for "subversive activities" from 1968 to 1975.

Much of the best contemporary writing from the mainland also follows in China's humanist tradition, including Yu Hua's (1960–) 余华 *To Live* 活着 (1992) and *Chronicle of a Blood Merchant* 许三观卖血记 (1995). And whereas Yu's portrait of a desperate father who nearly dies selling his blood offers a subtle critique of market capitalism, Yan Lianke's 阎连科 (1958–) *Dream of Ding Village* 丁庄梦 (2006) directly indicts the government's blood-selling profiteers who unleashed an AIDS epidemic in

Henan province. As Yan's characters die "like falling leaves," his haunting novel may be a twenty-first century version of Camus's *The Plague* (1947).

Pursuing progress

In *Bus Stop*, Glasses, refusing to waste his time merely waiting for the bus, studies English-language flashcards for his College Entrance Exam. He's tempted to walk but fears that a bus might come the moment they leave: "Maybe our waiting for a lifetime here, until old age and death, has been determined by fate. Why don't people create their own future? Why do we have to bitterly suffer as victims of fate?"

Gao's characters' plight recalls that of the sleepers Lu Xun hesitates to rouse in the preface to his first collection of stories, *Call to Arms* 呐喊 (1923). Likening China to "an iron house without windows, absolutely indestructible, with many people fast asleep inside who will soon die of suffocation," he fears that crying out would only torture those trapped. Yet when a friend insists that those awakened might destroy the iron house, Lu has a change of heart: "True, in spite of my own conviction, I could not blot out hope, for hope lies in the future."

Such hope for human-led progress departs from traditional conceptions of nature's cycles and heaven's will. Revolutionaries seek to reform political, economic, and social institutions because they believe that, unlike fate, these institutions can be changed. Committed to showing that injustice and suffering were caused by people with power rather than by destiny, Lu Xun, Mao Dun 茅盾 (1896–1981), and others founded the League of Left-Wing Writers in 1930.

Mao Dun's name (a *nom-de-plume*, and homophone for "contradiction") signaled his embrace of Marxism, and his fiction chronicles the structural contradictions crippling China's economy.

In "Spring Silkworms" 春蠶 (1932), a guileless peasant family's tender care of their silkworms yields abundant cocoons, but their superstitions blind them to the collapse of their market. And in Mao's naturalistic *Midnight* 子夜 (1933), a textile industrialist learns through successive losses the insufficiency of national capital to withstand foreign economic imperialism. Because portrayals of crushing socio-economic conditions argued for national revolution, leftists championed such realist fiction and drama. Realism's importance was confirmed by the *Compendium of Chinese New Literature* 中國新文學大系 (1935), a collection increasingly influential after the Japanese invasion (1937–45), the civil war, and CCP cultural policies restricted other sources.

Literature's subordination to progressive politics was decreed by the CCP leader Mao Zedong 毛泽东 (1893–1976) in his "Talks at the Yan'an Forum on Art and Literature" (1942). Determined to make China the vanguard of international Communism, Mao adapted Marxism to make land reform, class struggle, and mass rural mobilization the mainstays of his three decades of rule. Believing that the collective will of the people could transform China's material base, Mao viewed thought reform as key to the "revolutionary spirit" needed for a Communist utopia. To this end, the party nationalized publishing and regulated writers through the Chinese Writers' Association founded in 1953.

During the "seventeen years" between the birth of the PRC (1949) and the Cultural Revolution (1966–76), novels modeling Mao's collectivization programs became "how to" manuals for cadres facing recalcitrant former landlords or apathetic peasants. Winner of the 1951 Stalin Prize, Ding Ling's 丁铃 (1904–86) *The Sun Shines over the Sanggan River* 太阳照在桑干河上 (1948) drew on her personal experiences of land reform for its vivid characterizations and ominous depictions of violent vengeance.

A progressive vision persistently marked Mao-era historical novels, some of which still enjoy popular success, especially Yang

Mo's 杨沫 (1915–95) *Song of Youth* 青春之歌 (1958), which has sold more than five million copies in twenty languages. Set in the 1930s, her bildungsroman recounts the heroine's transformation from melancholic intellectual to devoted revolutionary. Upon reading Marxist theory, she embraces socialism: "From these books, she saw the future of the development of human society. From these books she saw the brilliant rays of truth and the road that she as an individual should take."

Works promoting socialist progress became dutifully optimistic after Mao launched his "Great Leap Forward" (1958–62), and his vice-minister of culture called for "revolutionary realism" and "revolutionary romanticism." In portraying a young mother's transformation from passivity to initiative, Ru Zhijuan's 茹志鹃 (1925–98) "Warmth of Spring" 春暖时节 (1959) exemplifies such ardent works. As an estranged couple bond over their efforts to engineer a crucial tool for the wife's work unit, the story highlights the overlapping benefits for the characters' personal and collective futures. The formulaic operas and ballets of "revolutionary model theater" further glorified self-sacrificing workers, soldiers, and peasants, as did collectivization novels such as Hao Ran's 浩然 (1932–2008) multivolume *Bright Sunny Days* 艳阳天 (1964–65) and *The Golden Road* 金光大道 (1972–74). Ignoring famines and environmental devastation, legacies of Mao's programs, these works presented visions of revolutionary history consistent with party policy and Mao's rising cult status.

During the "new period" of the post-Mao era, many writers supported the "four modernizations" of agriculture, industry, technology, and defense. Whereas the late Mao sought to strengthen the countryside, the CCP reform leader Deng Xiaoping 邓小平 (1904–97) emphasized industrialization and urbanization. "Reform literature" addressed the personal costs of modernization, as in Zhang Jie's 张洁 (1937–) *Leaden Wings* 沉重的翅膀 (1981), a psychological novel of parents devoted to duty and youths seeking personal fulfillment. Zhang was also one of the first writers to return to themes of romantic love, long forbidden during the Mao era. In her controversial "Love Cannot Be Forgotten" 爱, 是不能忘记的 (1979), the daughter-narrator's considerations of marriage frame her reading of her dead mother's diary. As she reads, its story of her mother's unrealized love for a married man inspires five views of marriage: a "commodity exchange," a social duty, and a means of procreation, but also potentially a loving relation, and a free choice. The story provoked impassioned discussions about the ethics of extramarital affairs in the face of culturally compelled marriage, and about socialism's progress in allowing young people to postpone marriage to find love.

After a revised constitution (1982) shifted emphasis from class struggle to economic development, the relaxation of thought control unleashed additional intense cultural debate and literary experimentation. Although still committed to "a socialist state under the people's democratic dictatorship," since the 1980s China has instituted market reforms promoting private enterprise; opened to foreign culture, technology, and capital; and generated the biggest building boom in history. Literature has traced this vertiginous, aggressive development. Neorealist and avant-garde works, and a growing body of reportage all reflect concerns about rising consumerism, massive rural-urban migration, environmental degradation, and China's threatened "humanitarian spirit."

China's development has also facilitated an explosion in entertainment culture, some of which reflects China's pursuit of both technological strength and cultural "soft power." Ever since Ye Yonglie's 叶永烈 (1940–) *Little Smart's Wandering in the Future* 小灵通漫游未来 (1978) sold more than 3 million copies (including the comic book version), China has become a leader in science fiction, now publishing the world's largest circulation sci-fi magazine, *Science Fiction World* 科幻世界. Much realist literature has also championed progressive social visions. At least since Lu Tianming's 陆天明 (1943–) trendsetting *Heaven Above* 苍天在上

(1995), popular anti-corruption novels have shaped perceptions of party reform, and literature on the Internet may also be raising expectations for socio-economic and political development.

Pursuing memory

When *Bus Stop* opened in Beijing in 1983, critics denounced Gao for abandoning socialist literature's progressive mandate. Despite the drama's authenticity in presenting the lives of ordinary people, it was attacked in the 1983 Anti-Spiritual Pollution Campaign. For when Glasses looks at his watch and announces "We've been here talking for a full ten years," his lament evokes the inescapable memory of China's devastating Cultural Revolution (1966–76). Designed to re-engineer people's beliefs by suppressing the "four olds" (traditional customs, culture, habits, and ideas), this crusade left millions dead as packs of young Red Guard zealots denounced their teachers and other professionals (breaking the fingers of artists and musicians), destroyed temples, and burned books and paintings. (Scholars estimate 3 million to 20 million deaths including deaths in labor camps and suicides.) As they paraded "class enemies" wearing humiliating placards and dunce's caps, insufficient fanaticism was deemed revisionism, so almost everyone colluded with persecutions, as Jung Chang 张戎 (1952–) later documented in her memoir *Wild Swans: Three Daughters of China* (1991).

During the political thaw following Mao's death and the fall of the Gang of Four (1976), brave writers began redressing the wounds of the Anti-Rightist Campaign (1957) and the Cultural Revolution. Even before the official relaxation of thought control, Lu Xinhua's 卢新华 (1954–) "Scar" 伤痕 (1978) and other works of "scar literature" testified to long-suppressed sorrow and compassion. In Zhang Jie's "Remorse" 忏悔 (1979), a man cowed by his expulsion from the party forbids his son to join a mass memorial service (an implicit protest of Mao's regime). After the son, his spirit broken, dies of an ordinary infection, the father's reinstatement in the

10. Decades after his death, Mao Zedong's image still watches over Tiananmen Square in Beijing.

party offers him little solace: "He had not even done the most basic thing: communicate to his dearest beloved son belief in truth." Guilt also plagues the protagonist of Dai Houying's 戴厚英 (1938–96) *Humanity, Oh Humanity* 人啊, 人！(1980, translated as *Stones of the Wall*). In her novel, multiple points of view and vivid flashbacks illustrate the piecemeal nature of memory and historical understanding. But as the classmate betrayed in 1957 consoles the protagonist in the narrative present, reconciling their histories opens the door to forgiveness and renewal.

On the heels of scar literature, other genres of testimony included "new realism," (pointedly distinct from "revolutionary realism"), "literature of reflection," and "prison literature," literally "big wall literature" 大墙文学, named after Cong Weixi's 从维熙 (1933–) "Red Magnolias Beneath the Wall" 大墙下的红玉兰 (1979). Despite decades of loyal military service, because of a few lines in his notebook criticizing Mao's deification, Cong's protagonist Ge Ling is summarily condemned to a life sentence of forced prison labor. Yet as in many works of prison literature, the protagonist experiences his incarceration as purifying, his ordeals strengthening his faith in the party and in Communism. Though he is shot dead while climbing a ladder to pick magnolias to make a wreath for the beloved premier Zhou Enlai, the novella ends with a "bright tail" when an old comrade escapes to Beijing to deliver the wreath stained red with Ling's blood. More shocking testimony about the labor camps came with Zhang Xianliang's 张贤亮 (1936–) semi-autobiographical *Half of Man Is Woman* 男人的一半是女人 (1985), in which sexual impotence becomes a telling effect of political repression.

Silenced for nearly four decades by Mao-era literary strictures, modernist works re-emerged and implicitly confronted the nation's collective historical traumas. Inspired by 1920s poets such as Wen Yiduo, young writers rekindled symbolism with "misty poetry," while "search-for-roots" fiction probed the sometimes pernicious legacies of culture and tradition. By looking backward and inward as well as forward and outward, these and other avant-garde works challenged the party's ideology of modernization. Historical determinism weighs heavily in many of these works, but they often portray decadence rather than progress.

By depicting historical periods before 1949, writers could exhume traumatic memories of the Cultural Revolution with less risk of censorship or reprisals. Influenced by the modernism of Kafka and Faulkner, along with the "magic realism" of Gabriel García Márquez, Mo Yan's 莫言 (1955–) *Red Sorghum* 红高粱家族 (1987) presents five overlapping (yet occasionally incongruous) accounts as the narrator, writing in 1985, imagines his grandparents' experiences during the brutal Japanese invasion of their village in 1939. Similar in its intense imagery and graphic violence, Su Tong's 苏童 (1963–) *My Life as Emperor* 我的帝王生涯 (1992) is set in an unspecified distant past, but the slicing out of concubines' tongues might remind readers of Cultural Revolution "struggle sessions" when Mao's Red Guards severed tongues to silence victims' loyal cries of "Long Live Chairman Mao!"

Recalling concerns about the destruction of nature and of ethnic minorities voiced in 1980s search-for-roots fiction, Jiang Rong's 姜戎 (1946–) best-selling *Wolf Totem* 狼图腾 (2004) provoked new concern over the devastation of Mongolia's fragile grasslands. Drawing on the author's experience as one of 12 million educated urban youth sent to learn from rural peasants during the Cultural Revolution, the novel recounts a "sent-down" youth's growing reverence for nomadic Mongolians and for the ecological balance symbolized by the wolf.

A comment on both collective amnesia and the creative yearnings of the soul, Ma Jian's 马建 (1953–) *Beijing Coma* 北京植物人 (originally titled *Land of Flesh* 肉土, 2008) follows the thoughts of its narrator-protagonist Dai Wei as he lies unconscious and paralyzed after a bullet to his head during the 1989 June Fourth Tiananmen Square protests. Formerly a PhD student in biology, Dai Wei lies in his mother's shabby Beijing apartment, relives the past, and ponders the present. When he awakens at the novel's end, his mother suffers a nervous breakdown as bulldozers begin to demolish their apartment. (Written after Ma's 1987 exile, the novel was published abroad before Chinese editions appeared in Hong Kong and Taiwan.)

The pursuit of memory (along with the powers and dangers of nostalgia) has also been central to fiction on Taiwan, especially in modernist works such as Bai Xianyong's 白先勇 (1937–) elegant story collection *Taipei People* 台北人 (1971). In the privileged world of Taipei's Shanghainese exiles depicted in Bai's "Eternal Snow Beauty" 永遠的尹雪艷 (1965), a seemingly enviable façade of genteel comfort soon reveals a forlorn vision of moral decadence. Sensual details of light, color, and fragrance shroud the beautiful hostess in mystery, but fantasies of recapturing the past ultimately doom her lovers and deny her own humanity. Since the lifting of martial law (1987), authors in Taiwan have also faced the ongoing ravages of the island's political traumas, as in Chen Yingzhen's *Zhao Nandong* 趙南棟 (1987). In this chilling account of Taiwan's "white terror," memories of a condemned political prisoner entrusting her infant son (Nandong) to a fellow prisoner are interwoven with the latter's search, thirty years later, to understand the now grown son's estrangement.

Pursuing pleasure

In *Bus Stop*, when Girl laments that she can't wear a certain trendy dress outside the city, Mom reassuringly strokes her hair. "Wear what you like. Don't wait until my age. You still count as youthful; some young guy will be attracted to you. You'll feel close, fall in love, and after you have his child, he'll become even more devoted." Surprisingly uncritical given her own dreary marriage, Mom's romantic idyll voices aspirations for personal happiness that were verboten during the Mao era's fanaticism for collective sacrifice. Yet both before and since the Mao period, longings for fulfillment through love, career, and material comforts rose dramatically.

While scholars often emphasize its ethics, Chinese literature has also long provided entertainment and pleasure. In contrast to the elite genres of history, philosophy, and poetry, much fiction and drama offered diversion and escapism to larger audiences, markets that soared after the 1875 introduction of less expensive Western printing techniques. As modern written Chinese further promoted literacy, a widening readership led to a proliferation of literary magazines, and *Saturday* 禮拜六 (1914–16, 1921–23), the best-selling periodical of popular fiction, reached a circulation of 50,000. Christened "Saturday fiction," sentimental romances, martial arts tales, detective stories, social satires, and "black curtain" accounts of scandals all flourished from the 1910s through the 1930s.

Such fiction was disparaged for distracting readers from national salvation, but avidly read. Though usually set in contemporary times, popular works generally spared readers the political issues posed by the critical realism of the period. Whereas leftist realist writers underscored economic determinism, many popular works present characters who exercise a self-determination that helps explain their appeal. In Zhang Henshui's 張恨水 (1895–1967) *Fate in Tears and Laughter* 啼笑因緣 (1930), the superhuman knight-errant Xiugu wins little mortal reward (she remains unmarried), but she exercises fantastical power in slaying a corrupt general, freeing his brutalized wife, and distributing his extravagant wealth to the poor.

Nor did all serious fiction follow the leftists' agenda for critical realism. Writers of the "Creation Society" championed the emotional expression of romanticism, while Shen Congwen 沉從文 (1902–88) wrote lyrical fiction celebrating nature, rustic customs, and other earthly enjoyments. Shen's pastoral novel *Border Town* 邊城 (1934) uses bucolic imagery to recount the mutual love between an elderly ferryman and his granddaughter, whom he tries to protect as she comes of age. Pursuits of pleasure and sensuality also overshadow concerns about social problems in the modernist works of the Shanghai-based "New Sensationists."

These works, influenced by Freudian psychoanalysis, foreground sexuality and self-consciousness, as in Shi Zhicun's 施蟄存 (1905–2003) story of an office worker's fantasies about a young woman in "One Evening in the Rainy Season" 梅雨之夕 (1929).

Obsession with sensual gratification, often linked to struggles for power or wealth, also haunts the desolate characters of Zhang Ailing's 張愛玲 (1920–95) incisive masterpieces, many set during the wartime Japanese occupation of Shanghai and Hong Kong. In her *Love in a Fallen City* 傾城之戀 (1943), a young divorcée's desperation for the financial security of marriage leaves her suitor skeptical of her love, but the couple discovers unexpected contentment as they survive the bombing of Hong Kong. In "Lust, Caution" 色, 戒 (1979) a former student actress sent to seduce a collaborator falls in love and warns him of the plot to assassinate him, for which he executes her and her comrades.

Often likened to Zhang Ailing, Wang Anyi 王安忆 (1954–) confronts the potentially destructive forces of sexual desire in a trilogy of lyrical novellas. In her *Love on a Barren Mountain* 荒山之恋 (1986), a sensitive cellist and his strong-willed mistress pursue an extramarital affair, and its exposure leads to their double suicide. *Love in a Small Town* 小城之恋 (1986) offers a visceral account of the erotic awakening, shame, and sexual aggression of two young dancers, and *Love in a Brocade Valley* 锦绣谷之恋 (1987) contrasts an editor's lackluster marriage with her wistful desire for an inaccessible writer. The fleeting rewards of material pleasures are shown in *Song of Everlasting Sorrow* 长恨歌 (1995), Wang's prizewinning novel about a beauty whose early fame in magazines and near-win in the 1946 Miss Shanghai contest ill prepare her to endure four decades of political tumult.

After the government slashed subsidies for publishers in the mid-1980s, many presses turned to popular literature, including gangster fiction by the self-proclaimed "hooligan" Wang Shuo 王朔 (1958–) and "body writing" by "glamour girl writers" such as

Mian Mian 棉棉 (1970–) and Wei Hui 卫慧 (1973–). In the decade between Wang Shuo's *Playing for Thrills* 玩儿的就是心跳 (1989) and Wei Hui's *Shanghai Baby* 上海宝贝 (1999), novels banned in China (but published in Taiwan and circulated underground) also explored political and sexual deviance. Hong Ying's 虹影 (1962–) *Summer of Betrayal* 背叛之夏 (originally titled *The Generation of Naked Dancers* 裸舞代, 1992), set in the shadow of the 1989 June Fourth incident, confronts the moral implications of membership in the "Degraded Survivors' Club" as the protagonist uses her sexuality (e.g., taking multiple partners at a final party) to further her quest for selfhood.

Preoccupation with private pleasures also marks much of the fiction written in Hong Kong, both among émigré writers such as Liu Yichang 劉以鬯 (1918–) and among Hong Kong natives. Ruled by the British for 156 years (1841–1997), Hong Kong enjoyed considerable press freedoms, but self-censorship fostered apolitical writing focusing on private lives. Liu's story "Intersection" 對倒 (1972) alternates between the ruminations of a young woman and a middle-aged émigré whose paths cross in a movie theater. While the émigré reflects on his vanished life in Shanghai and the changes he has witnessed during his twenty years in Hong Kong, the young woman, aroused by an explicit photograph, projects her face onto mannequins, singers, and movie stars. The story ends with the characters' parallel erotic dreams, her fantasy of a handsome lover conjoining with his memory of his virile youth.

Pursuing "cultural China"

Despite its critical dialogues, Gao's *Bus Stop* ends hopefully. A romance seems to be budding between Glasses and Girl, and all the characters set off together on foot. Hothead carries Mom's heavy bag as she supports Gramps, and even Director Ma, earlier the least willing, calls out for the others to wait. This ending affirms values of social responsibility, as well as visions of China joining an increasingly modernized world.

Because Gao himself did not wait, but left China in 1987 and took French citizenship before his 2000 Nobel Prize in Literature, his award has been harshly criticized. Contention over Gao's prize, seen by some as an affront to resident Chinese writers, intensified debates about the boundaries and political uses of Chinese literature. These debates had already led some to champion the notion of a greater "cultural China" not limited by the political borders of the PRC.

Those eager not to let geopolitics restrict discussions of Chinese literature sometimes invoke the term "Sinophone" to include literature written in Chinese by writers in the Asian and wider diaspora. Sinophone may be an apt label for a global audience of Chinese-language readers. It may also appeal to those seeking Chinese cultural values, such as the discipline and traditionalism idealized in the martial arts novels of Hong Kong's Jin Yong 金庸 (1924–), probably the most widely read living Chinese author. Yet the term "Sinophone" may strain to encompass literature written in Taiwanese, other topolects, or other languages.

Thanks to dedicated translators (whose labors of love are seldom lucrative), publishers are slowly bringing out translations of the many deserving Chinese works. Yet as Chinese authors writing in English and French have garnered major awards, for much of the world these writers have come to represent transnational Chinese literature. Many readers have learned about the Cultural Revolution from Dai Sijie 戴思杰 (1954–), who has lived in France since 1984 but drew on his experience as a "sent-down" youth for his international bestseller *Balzac et la Petite Tailleuse chinoise* (2000, *Balzac and the Little Chinese Seamstress*, 2001). In recounting its young protagonists' discovery of a forbidden cache of nineteenth-century French novels, Dai's heartrending tale demonstrates literature's power for personal transformation, even in the face of manipulation or repression.

Americans in particular now buy more books written in English by Chinese-born authors than translations from Chinese. Ha Jin 哈金 (1956–), who published his first book of poetry in English just five years after his 1985 emigration, rose to fame with his spare novel *Waiting* (1999), which recounts a man's devastating discovery after his eighteen-year wait for a divorce. More recently, Yiyun Li 李翊云 (1972–), who came to Iowa to study immunology before turning to writing, has penned startling stories, many on the blessings and limitations of love. Collected in *A Thousand Years of Good Prayers* (2005) and *Gold Boy, Emerald Girl* (2010), Li's stories increasingly depict Chinese living in America, and her relative youth means that her identity as "Chinese" may change to "Chinese-American." Yet literature transcends taxonomies that would put people into boxes, and this integral power of literary culture promises a compelling future for the living tradition of Chinese literature.

References

Chapter 1

Lu Ji, "Looking down . . . ," from "Rhymeprose on Literature: *The Wen-fu of Lu Chi*," trans. Achilles Fang, *Harvard Journal of Asiatic Studies* 14 (1951): 546.

"THE RECEPTIVE brings about sublime success . . . ," from *The I Ching or Book of Changes,* trans. Richard Wilhelm and Cary F. Baynes (Princeton, NJ: Princeton University Press, 1967), 11.

Confucius, last of four quotations from the *Analects*: "To know it . . . ," trans. Wing-Tsit Chan, *A Source Book in Chinese Philosophy* (Princeton, NJ: Princeton University Press, 1963), 30.

Zhuangzi on emotions, *Readings in Chinese Literary Thought,* trans. Stephen Owen (Cambridge, MA: Council on East Asian Studies, Harvard University Press, 1992), 327.

Chapter 2

Translations for most of the poetic modes are modeled on Stephen Owen, "The Twenty-Four Categories of Poetry," *Readings in Chinese Literary Thought*, 303–50.

Anonymous, "Selections from 'Nineteen Old Poems of the Han,'" trans. Burton Watson, *The Columbia Book of Chinese Poetry: From Early Times to the Thirteenth Century* (New York: Columbia University Press, 1984), 96–97, slightly revised by Sabina Knight.

Final line of "Nineteen Old Poems II," trans. Stephen Owen, *An Anthology of Chinese Literature: Beginnings to 1911* (New York: Norton, 1996), 259.

Wang Wei, "Deer Fence," trans. Stephen Owen, *Anthology of Chinese Literature*, 393.

Chapter 3

Zuo's Commentary, "You have a mother . . . ," trans. Burton Watson, in
Columbia Anthology of Traditional Chinese Literature, ed. Victor
H. Mair (New York: Columbia University Press, 1994), 517.

Discourses of the States, "He who serves . . . ," trans. Cyril Birch,
Anthology of Chinese Literature, vol. 1, *From Early Times to the
Fourteenth Century* (New York: Grove Press, 1965), 35.

Sima Qian, "Letter to Jen An (Shao-ch'ing)," trans. Birch, *Anthology of
Chinese Literature*, vol. 1, 101, slightly revised by Sabina Knight.

Pu Songling, *Strange Stories from a Chinese Studio*, trans. John Minford
(London: Penguin Classics, 2006), "If ghosts and foxes . . . ," 228;
"Wise Counsel! . . ," 215; "We are all foxes . . . ," 84; and "Huangfu
and Grace . . . ," 86.

Chapter 4

Lines from "Tang Xianzu's *The Peony Pavilion*," trans. Cyril Birch,
Scenes for Mandarins: The Elite Theater of the Ming (New York:
Columbia University Press, 1995), 156, 157, 158, 160, passim.

K'ung Shang-jen, *The Peach Blossom Fan (T'ao-hua-shan)*, trans.
Chen Shih-hsiang and Harold Acton, with Cyril Birch (Berkeley:
University of California Press, 1976), 297–98.

Cao Xueqin, "As flowers fall . . . ," *The Story of the Stone*, vol. 1, *The
Golden Days*, trans. David Hawkes (Harmondsworth: Penguin,
1973), 467.

Chapter 5

Liang Qichao, "On the Relationship between Fiction and the
Government of the People," trans. Gek Nai Cheng, in *Modern
Chinese Literary Thought: Writings on Literature 1893–1945*, ed.
Kirk A. Denton (Stanford, CA: Stanford University Press, 1996), 74.

Wen Yiduo, "Dead Water," trans. Kai-yu Hsu, in *Twentieth Century
Chinese Poetry: An Anthology* (Garden City, NY: Doubleday,
1963), 61.

Wu Zuxiang, "Young Master Gets His Tonic," trans. Cyril Birch, in *The
Columbia Anthology of Modern Chinese Literature*, 2nd ed., ed.
Joseph S. M. Lau and Howard Goldblatt (New York: Columbia

University Press, 2007), "What a wonderful world . . . ," 153; "Everything around here . . . ," 157.

Lu Xun, "A Madman's Diary," trans. Yang Xianyi and Gladys Yang, in *Columbia Anthology,* ed. Lau and Goldblatt, 15, 16.

Ye Shaojun, "A Posthumous Son," trans. Bonnie S. McDougall, in *Columbia Anthology,* ed. Lau and Goldblatt, 27.

Lu Xun, "Preface," trans. Yang Xianyi and Gladys Yang, in *Columbia Anthology*, ed. Lau and Goldblatt, 6.

Yang Mo, *Song of Youth,* trans. Sabina Knight, in *The Heart of Time: Moral Agency in Twentieth-Century Chinese Fiction* (Cambridge, MA: Harvard University Asia Center, 2006), 146.

Zhang Jie, "Remorse," trans. Helen F. Siu and Zelda Stern, in *Mao's Harvest: Voices from China's New Generation* (New York: Oxford University Press, 1983), 29.

Further reading

General works

Idema, Wilt, and Lloyd Half. *A Guide to Chinese Literature*. Ann Arbor: Center for Chinese Studies, University of Michigan, 1997.

Lévy, André. *Chinese Literature, Ancient and Classical*. Translated by William H. Nienhauser Jr. Bloomington: Indiana University Press, 2000.

Mair, Victor H., ed. *The Columbia History of Chinese Literature*. New York: Columbia University Press, 2002.

Nienhauser, William H. Jr., ed. *The Indiana Companion to Traditional Chinese Literature*. 2 vols. Bloomington: Indiana University Press, 1986, 1998.

General anthologies

Birch, Cyril, ed. *Anthology of Chinese Literature*. 2 vols. New York: Grove Press, 1965, 1972, rpt. 1994. An astute anthology of classics.

Idema, Wilt, and Beata Grant, eds. *The Red Brush: Writing Women of Imperial China*. Cambridge, MA: Harvard University Asia Center, 2004. A broad history of women's writing with generous examples and excerpts from diverse genres.

Mair, Victor H., ed. *The Columbia Anthology of Traditional Chinese Literature*. New York: Columbia University Press, 1996.

Mair, Victor H., ed. *The Shorter Columbia Anthology of Traditional Chinese Literature*. New York: Columbia University Press, 2000. Both anthologies provide a broad range of texts with thorough introductions and notes.

Mair, Victor H., Nancy S. Steinhardt, and Paul R. Goldin, eds. *Hawai'i Reader in Traditional Chinese Culture*. Honolulu: University of

Hawai'i Press, 2005. Introductory essays and 92 primary texts, many from sources beyond traditional literary canons.

Minford, John, and Joseph S. M. Lau, eds. *Classical Chinese Literature: An Anthology of Translations*. Vol. 1, *From Antiquity to the Tang Dynasty*. New York: Columbia University Press; Hong Kong: The Chinese University Press, 2000. Classic translations of over 1,000 selections.

Owen, Stephen, ed. and trans. *An Anthology of Chinese Literature: Beginnings to 1911*. New York: W. W. Norton, 1996. Heavily weighted toward poetry; selections and commentary bring out conversations between texts.

Chapter 1: Foundations

Wing-Tsit Chan. *A Source Book in Chinese Philosophy*. Princeton, NJ: Princeton University Press, 1963. Helpful introductions and well chosen excerpts.

Dale, Corinne H., ed. *Chinese Aesthetics and Literature: A Reader*. Albany: State University of New York Press, 2004. Introductory essays by major scholars.

de Bary, Wm. Theodore, and Irene Bloom, eds. *Sources of Chinese Tradition*. Vol. 1, *From Earliest Times to 1600*, 2nd ed. New York: Columbia University Press, 1999. A classic text with authoritative introductions and extended excerpts.

de Bary, Wm. Theodore, and Richard Lufrano, eds. *Sources of Chinese Tradition*. Vol. 2, *From 1600 Through the Twentieth Century*, 2nd ed. New York: Columbia University Press, 1999. An authoritative text updated through the late twentieth century.

Ivanhoe, Philip J., and Bryan W. Van Norden, eds. *Readings in Classical Chinese Philosophy*, 2nd ed. Indianapolis: Hackett Publishing, 2005. Selected readings from Confucius, Mencius, Zhuangzi, Xunzi, and others, as well as a general introduction.

Chapter 2: Poetry and poetics

Kang-i Sun Chang, and Haun Saussy, eds. *Women Writers of Traditional China: An Anthology of Poetry and Criticism*. Stanford, CA: Stanford University Press, 1999. Poems from the Han to the early twentieth century, as well as prefaces, biographies, and criticism by and about women writers.

Chaves, Jonathan, ed. and trans. *The Columbia Book of Later Chinese Poetry: Yüan, Ming, and Ch'ing Dynasties (1279–1911)*. New York:

Columbia University Press, 1989. Translations and biographical sketches of 42 poets, with paintings.

Owen, Stephen. *Readings in Chinese Literary Thought*. Cambridge, MA: Council on East Asian Studies, Harvard University Press, 1992. Translations with commentary and original Chinese of seven full texts and many excerpts from earliest eras through the Qing dynasty.

Owen, Stephen. *Traditional Chinese Poetry and Poetics: Omen of the World*. Madison: University of Wisconsin Press, 1985. The most seminal of Owen's important critical works.

Watson, Burton, ed. and trans. *The Columbia Book of Chinese Poetry: From Early Times to the Thirteenth Century*. New York: Columbia University Press, 1984. 420 poems by 96 poets, with helpful introductions and focus on major poets.

Chapter 3: Classical narrative

Campany, Robert Ford. *Strange Writing: Anomaly Accounts in Early Medieval China*. Albany: State University of New York Press, 1996. A scholarly introduction to records of the strange.

Xiao Tong (comp.). *Wen xuan, or Selections of Refined Literature*. Translated and annotated by David R. Knechtges. 3 vols. (more projected). Princeton, NJ: Princeton University Press, 1982, 1987, 1996. Translations of diverse genres.

Ssu-ma Ch'ien. *The Grand Scribe's Records*. Edited by William H. Nienhauser Jr. Translated by Nienhauser et al. 9 vols. Bloomington: Indiana University Press, 1994–2010. Full scholarly translation with extensive footnotes.

Ma, Y. W., and Joseph S. M. Lau, eds. *Traditional Chinese Stories: Themes and Variations*. New York: Columbia University Press, 1978, rpt., Boston: Cheng and Tsui Co., 1986. 61 translations, arranged thematically, of many genres, from early histories and jottings to tales of the marvelous and vernacular stories.

Pu Songling. *Strange Tales from a Chinese Studio*. Translated by John Minford. London: Penguin Classics, 2006. Charming translations of selected stories.

Chapter 4: Vernacular drama and fiction

Birch, Cyril. *Scenes for Mandarins: The Elite Theater of the Ming*. New York: Columbia University Press, 1995. Translations of excerpts from and engaging commentaries on six masterpieces of Ming drama.

Cao Xueqin. *The Story of the Stone.* Translated by David Hawkes and John Minford. 5 vols. Harmondsworth: Penguin, 1973–1986. Elegant rendering of the novel better known as *Dream of the Red Chamber.*

Hsia, C. T. *The Classic Chinese Novel: A Critical Introduction.* New York: Columbia University Press, 1968, rpt., Bloomington: Indiana University Press, 1980, rpt., Ithaca: Cornell University Press, 1996. Chapters on each of six masterpieces.

Plaks, Andrew, ed. *Chinese Narrative: Critical and Theoretical Essays.* Princeton, NJ: Princeton University Press, 1977. Seminal scholarly essays.

Rolston, David L., ed. *How to Read the Chinese Novel.* Princeton, NJ: Princeton University Press, 1990. A scholarly introduction to the commentary tradition.

Wang Shifu. *The Story of the Western Wing.* Edited and translated by Stephen H. West and Wilt L. Idema. Berkeley: University of California Press, 1995. A complete translation with an informative introduction.

Chapter 5: Modern literature

Xiaomei Chen, ed. *The Columbia Anthology of Modern Chinese Drama.* New York: Columbia University Press, 2010. Critical introduction and translations of 22 plays from 1919 to 2000 from the PRC, Hong Kong, and Taiwan.

Hsia, C. T. *A History of Modern Chinese Fiction.* 1st ed. New Haven, CT: Yale University Press, 1961. 3rd ed. Bloomington: Indiana University Press, 1999. A classic critical introduction.

Lau, Joseph S. M., and Howard Goldblatt, eds. *The Columbia Anthology of Modern Chinese Literature.* New York: Columbia University Press, 2nd ed., 2007. Well-translated stories, poems, and essays.

McDougall, Bonnie S., and Kam Louie. *The Literature of China in the Twentieth Century.* New York: Columbia University Press, 1997. Brief entries on major authors' poetry, fiction, and drama, divided into three periods from 1900 to 1989.

Mostow, Joshua, ed. *The Columbia Companion to Modern East Asian Literature.* New York: Columbia University Press, 2003. Essays on major movements, authors, and genres from Japan, China, and Korea.

Websites

The Association for Asian Studies
www.aasianst.org
Links to web resources for scholars and students of Asian studies. For
China links see *www.aasianst.org/links/wwwchina.htm*

The China Gateway
www.bc.edu/research/chinagateway
Run by Professor Rebecca Nedostup of Boston College, this site points
to a broad collection of resources; for language study and literature
see *www.bc.edu/research/chinagateway/culthist/langlit.html*

Chinese Bibliography Database
https://chinesebib.sas.upenn.edu
Run by the Department of East Asian Languages and Civilizations,
University of Pennsylvania, a thorough and regularly updated
online bibliography.

MCLC Resource Center
http://mclc.osu.edu
Run by Professor Kirk A. Denton of Ohio State University in
conjunction with the journal *Modern Chinese Literature and
Culture,* this indispensable site contains book reviews, publications,
and an extensive database of bibliographies of mostly English-
language translations, studies, and other reference works of and on
modern and contemporary Chinese literature.

Renditions

www.cuhk.edu.hk/rct/renditions/index.html

Run by The Chinese University of Hong Kong, this site includes a database of authors, translators, and titles published by this journal and press devoted to English translations of Chinese literature.

Index

G

H

I

J

K

L